S0-BRE-300

World Chronology Series

CANADA

A CHRONOLOGY AND FACT BOOK

875-1973

Compiled and Edited by
BRIAN H. W. HILL

1973
OCEANA PUBLICATIONS, INC
Dobbs Ferry, New York

Library of Congress Cataloging in Publication Data

Hill, Brian H   W
    Canada, 875-1973: a chronology & fact book.

    (World chronology series)
    Bibliography: p
    1. Canada--History--Chronology. 2. Canada--
History--Sources. I. Title.
F1006.H54   971   73-7929
ISBN 0-379-16307-1

Manufactured in the United States of America

TABLE OF CONTENTS

EDITOR'S FOREWORD

Although any chronology is selective, one which attempts to present a subject of such scope as the history of Canada must necessarily be an extremely arbitrary selection of facts. With that in mind, the following is a collection of dates from Canadian history considered to be of some historical consequence in the shaping of the modern Canadian nation. The presentation is objective, allowing as little comment as possible, and meant to be a source for reference rather than a history. The only organization is chronological as this is more useful than a more thematic presentation under subject headings, as all previous similar studies of Canadian history have been. There is some regard to natural development, however, and facts have been selected with some general thematic criteria in mind, such as developing autonomy, etc.

The documents included are also meant as reference material and are presented with little additional comment. It should be noted that the British North America Act is that one which passed through the British parliament in 1867. This Act has been amended significantly several times since then.

The selected bibliography will be of use for further explication of any event given in either the chronology or the documents. It represents a random sampling of material on different aspects of a very broad and complex topic. Most of the items in the bibliography are available in paperback editions or are standard works. Many also have good bibliographies on specific areas.

This chronology is up-to-date as of May, 1973.

Brian H. W. Hill

PRE-1600   EXPLORATION

c. 875   It has been theorized that Celt-Irish monks from Iceland
            settled on Cape Breton Island but were gradually ab-
            sorbed by the native Micmac population and the settle-
            ment died out.

982   Eric the Red from Iceland is claimed to have landed on
            Baffin Island.

986   Bjarni Herjulfsson, from Iceland, is thought to have
            sailed along eastern coast from Newfoundland (Vinland
            or Wineland) to Labrador (Markland or Forest land) to
            Baffin Island (Helluland or Story land).

1004   Lief Ericson, from Greenland, spent winter of 1004 - 5
            at L'Anse au Meadow, Newfoundland.

1005-8   Thorwald Ericson, from Greenland, and brother of Lief,
            spent two winters in Newfoundland and was killed there.

1012-16   Thorfinn Karlsefni, from Greenland and husband of
            Thorwald's widow, spent three winters in Newfoundland.
            His son, Snorre, was born there in 1013, being probably
            the first white child born in North America. The settle-
            ment was eventually abandoned.

1497   June 24. Giovanni Caboto, A Genoese, sailed from
            Bristol in Mathew. He landed on Cape Breton Island at
            Cape St. George and claimed it for Henry VII of England.
            It is believed by some that it was Cape Bonavista which
            he sighted.

c. 1498   Devonshire fishermen began to fish around Newfoundland.
            They were joined by Portuguese fishermen in 1501, the
            French in 1502, and the Spanish in 1545. Until 1583 the
            island was free to all with no country claiming sovereign-
            ty.

1522   Wintering crews were left behind to cut timber for build-
            ings and boats to serve the fishing fleet. The first
            settlements were made between Cape St. Francis and
            Cape Race and around Conception Bay. From the start,
            St. John's was the center of fishing and trading on the
            island.

1524   Giovanni de Verrazano, a Florentine sailing from St. Malo, explored the Atlantic coast from Florida to Newfoundland. He named the land, Francesca, after his sponsor, Francis I of France.

1534   May 10. Jacques Cartier, a Breton, sailing for the French, started off from St. Malo. He sailed around the northern tip of Newfoundland and down west coast of the island.

June 29. Cartier sighted Prince Edward Island and explored the north and west shores.

July 24. Cartier landed at Penouille Point, at the entrance of Gaspé, and claimed it for France.

1535   August 10. Cartier returned for a second trip and entered the estuary of the St. Lawrence, determined to find the three Indian kingdoms which he had been told of the year before by the Indians of the Gaspé.

September 16. Cartier reached the Iroquois village of Stadacona (Quebec City).

October 2. Cartier reached the Huron village of Hochelaga (Montreal), where he wintered. The next spring he returned to France with Donacona, a Huron chief, who died in France before Cartier could organize a return voyage.

1541   January 15. Jean François de la Rocque, Seigneur de Roberval was named lieutenant-general of the new territory that Cartier had discovered. Roberval was granted seigneurial ownership and retained Cartier as captain-general and master pilot to establish a settlement.

August. Cartier prepared to winter at Cape Rouge near Stadacona (Quebec City) and named his settlement Charlesbourg-Royal.

1542   June 8. Cartier, returning to France, met Roberval at St. John's, Newfoundland.

July. Roberval reached Cartier's settlement near Stadacona. He returned to France with the colonists who had accompanied him out, in September 1543.

1576   Martin Frobisher made his first voyage to Baffin Island for the Russia Company.

1577   Martin Frobisher made his second voyage to Baffin Island this time with the Cathay Company.

1578   Martin Frobisher made his third voyage to Baffin Island again for the Cathay Company.

With the aid of Sir Walter Raleigh, Sir Humphrey Gilbert obtained a charter from Queen Elizabeth of England, conveying to him large tracts of land in the new world, including the island of Newfoundland. He was allowed six years to establish a viable claim and served as governor from 1578 to 1583.

1583   August 5. Gilbert claimed Newfoundland for England at St. John's harbour. He was lost at sea on November 9, 1583 while returning home.

Summer. Spanish fishing fleet off Newfoundland captured by English during war between Elizabeth and Philip II of Spain. The Spanish never returned to the fishing grounds.

1585-7   John Davis made three voyages to Davis Strait for the North West Company. He described Hudson Strait in August 1587, and reached latitude 72° 12' North, which he named Sanderson's Hope.

1598   January 12. Troilus de Mesquoat, Marquis de la Roche was appointed lieutenant-general of Canada, Newfoundland and Labrador, and given ownership and a monopoly of trade, provided that he found a colony. De la Roche landed a colony on Sable Island and then returned to France. The colony returned in 1603.

1600-1700   FIRST SETTLEMENTS

1599   November 22. François de Pont-Gravé, merchant of St. Malo, and Pierre Chauvin, sea captain, were granted a ten-year monopoly of the fur trade, provided they sent out colonists.

1600-1   Chauvin attempted a settlement at Tadoussac in the winter but failed. Chauvin then died in 1603.

1602	February. Commander Aymar de Chastes was named lieutenant-general of New France by Henry IV.
1603	Summer. De Chastes formed a trading company under Du Pont-Gravé and he and Samuel Champlain traded as far as Hochelaga.
	November 8. Pierre du Guast, Sieur de Monts, was named lieutenant-general in Acadie by Henry IV.
1604	De Monts, accompanied by Champlain and the Sieur de Poutrincourt, visited Acadie. He granted the Port Royal site (Annapolis, N.S.) to Poutrincourt and made a settle-ment for himself on St. Croix Isle off the coast of Maine This colony then moved to Port Royal in the summer of 1605 and De Monts returned to France.
1607	De Monts concession was cancelled, but he managed to obtain a one year trading concession on January 7, 1608 and was named lieutenant-general of New France.
1608	July 3. Samuel Champlain, sent to New France as De Monts' lieutenant, founded Quebec City.
1610	May 2. James I of England granted a charter to Alder-man John Guy's company to colonize Newfoundland from Cape St. Mary's to Cape Bonavista.
	Winter. Henry Hudson, in the Discovery, was in James Bay for the Muscovy Company of London. He wintered there and the next spring his crew mutinied and set him adrift on June 21, 1611. His fate is unknown.
1611	After his trading concession had been cancelled once more, De Monts turned his attention to the St. Lawrence valley. He ceded what rights he had left in Acadie to Antoinette de Pons, Marquise de Guercheville.
	October 8. Louis de Bourbon, Comte de Soissons, was named governor and lieutenant-general of New France by his nephew, Louis XIII. He received seignural rights and a trading monopoly. Champlain was appointed his deputy and commander at Quebec. De Soissons died on November 12, 1611.

November 22. Henry de Bourbon, Prince de Condé, was named viceroy of New France and received the trade monopoly. He retained Champlain as his lieutenant.

1612   August 27. Sir Thomas Button, sailing for the English, wintered at the mouth of the Nelson River which he named.

1613   The Marquise de Guercheville put Captain La Saussaye in charge of an expedition which founded a Jesuit mission on St. Sauveur (Mount Desert Isle). The mission was razed by the English in October.

1614   Champlain organized the trading group known as the Company of Merchants of Rouen and St. Malo, who agreed to send out colonists.

1615-16   William Baffin, in the Discovery, was sent by an English company to explore the northern reaches of the new world. He named Sir Thomas Smith Sound, Sir Francis Jones Sound, and Sir James Lancaster Sound and reached latitude 76^0 north in 1616.

1620   February 25. Henri, Duc de Montmorency, Admiral of France, bought out Henry de Bourbon, Prince de Condé and was appointed Viceroy of New France, the position formerly held by the Prince. Champlain was retained as lieutenant in Quebec.

November 8. Montmorency cancelled the trading concession of the Company of Merchants, replacing it with a company formed by Guillaume de Caen.

1621   September 10. A grant, including Nova Scotia, New Brunswick, and the Gaspé Peninsula, was made to a Scottish nobleman named Sir William Alexander by James I of England. Alexander named the area, Nova Scotia (New Scotland). His first attempt at a settlement in the winter of 1621-2 failed.

1623   February 4. Feudalism begins in New France with the grant of a fief at Sault-au-Matelot to Louis Hébert by Montmorency.

1624   Charles de Biencourt, son and heir of Poutrincourt, died in Acadie in 1624, designating Charles de la Tour as his heir. La Tour abandoned Port Royal and settled at a post called Fort Laméron, on Cape Sable renaming it Fort Saint Louis.

1627   April 29. The trading charter of Guillaume de Caen was
            revoked by Cardinal Richelieu and the Company of New
            France or the Company of One Hundred Associates, was
            formed.

            Summer. Sir William Alexander disembarked some
            English settlers at the abandoned Port Royal and erected
            a post called Scots Fort or Charles Fort.

1629   August 9. Quebec was captured by the English under
            Admiral David Kirke and was controlled by a garrison
            under Lewis Kirke, during the war between England and
            France.

            October 6. The La Tour and Alexander families, trad-
            ing rivals in Acadie, came to an agreement on joint
            ownership of the area.

1632   March 10. Isaac de Razilly was appointed lieutenant-
            general for the entire province of Acadie by Louis XIII.

            March 23. By the treaty of St. Germaine-en-Laye, the
            English gave up their claim to Acadie in favour of the
            French.

            April 20. Razilly was appointed lieutenant-general of
            all New France. Champlain and LaTour were nominally
            under his command at Quebec and Fort St. Louis.

            July 13. The French re-occupied Quebec.

            September 8. Razilly settled at Le Havre, naming it
            Port Ste. Marie-de-Grace. He received the surrender
            of Acadie from the English, under Captain Andrew
            Forester at Charles Fort (Port Royal) in December.

1633   March 1. Samuel Champlain was appointed lieutenant-
            general of New France by Richelieu. He died in office
            December 25, 1635.

1634   Jean Nicolet explored Lake Michigan and Trois Riviéres
            was founded by La Biolette. Trois Riviéres soon became
            the fur trading center of New France.

1635   November. Charles de Menon, Sieur d'Aulnay-Charisnay,
            and Charles Amador de la Tour were appointed joint

lieutenant-generals of Acadie. Eventually civil war broke out between them. La Tour was recalled but then reinstated once again when de Menon died on May 24, 1650.

1642   May 18. Ville Marie de Montreal was founded by Paul de Chomeday, Sieur de Mainsonneuve, who served as governor of Ville Marie (Montreal) until removed by the Marquis de Tracy in 1665.

1643   August 3. Iroquois hostilities against the French began with the capture and torture of Father Isaac Joque at Lac St. Pierre.

1645   March 6. The King's Council ratified an agreement whereby the Company of One Hundred Associates would sublet the fur trading monopoly to residents of the colony. They retained for themselves the seignural ownership of the land, however. The colonial company organized by this agreement was called the Compagnie des Habitants.

1647   March 27. The Company of One Hundred Associates was further reorganized when Louis XIV issued an edict setting up the Council of Quebec. This council was to be composed of the governor of Quebec, the superior of the Jesuits until a bishop should arrive, and the governor of Montreal. It was to govern the country on behalf of the company in all matters of finance, fur trade and general policy. Representatives from Quebec, Montreal and Trois Riviéres were entitled to attend meetings and to express their sentiments.

1654   July 27. The English, under Robert Sedgewick, captured Fort St. John and La Tour was taken to London. There, he sold his interest in Acadie to William Crowne and Sir Thomas Temple, fur traders, on September 20, 1656. La Tour then returned to Acadie where he died in 1663. Sir Thomas Temple meanwhile was appointed governor of Acadie by Oliver Cromwell.

1659   Pierre Esprit Radisson and Médard Chouart des Groseilliers had reached the upper Mississippi area and by 1661 had reached James Bay.

June 8. François de Montmorency, Monseigneur de Laval arrived in Quebec as acting bishop of Quebec and vicar-apostolic in New France.

1661 The Royal Navy assigned a war ship to the Newfoundland station to escort the English fishing fleet to and from the fishing grounds.

1663 February 24. The Company of One Hundred Associates conveyed to the French Crown all their interests in Canada, making New France a Royal Colony.

March 21. In an edict, Louis XIV revoked all grants made by the Company of One Hundred Associates of lands which had not been cleared six months after the date of the grant.

April. By the Edit de Création du Conseil Souverain, authority in New France was vested in a Sovereign Council (in 1703 the name was changed to the Superior Council). This council consisted of primarily three men. The governor was the political and military head, being the King's representative in the colony and thus held the most power in reality. The other two members were the bishop of Quebec who was the spiritual head and the intendant, who was the head of administration. Advice was furnished by five councilors selected by the governor and the bishop.

1664 May. In an edict, Louis XIV established La Compaigne des Indies Occidentales to carry on trade in New France. This company was discontinued ten years later by the edict of December 1674.

1665 March 23. Jean Talon was appointed intendant. His term lasted from September 23, 1665 until October 22, 1668.

June 30. Alexandre de Prouville, Marquis de Tracy, arrived with the Carignan-Saliere Regiment to remove the Mohawk-Iroquois menace. He served as Lieutenant-general in the French colonies of North America from 1663 to 1667.

1667 July 31. The Treaty of Breda returned Acadie to the French but they did not occupy it until 1670.

1668	September 29. Médard Chouart des Groseilliers in the <u>Nonsuch</u> sailed to the mouth of the Rupert River. He built Fort Charles and wintered there.
1669	May 14. Jean Talon was reappointed as intendant. His term extended from September 23, 1670 until October 1672.
1670	May 2. A charter was signed by Charles II of England, providing for a trading monopoly for the Company of Adventurers of England Trading into Hudson's Bay.
	September 8. Charles Bayly was appointed the first "Hudson's Bay Company" governor before the charter was signed. He arrived at Fort Charles with Radisson and Groseilliers on September 8 and made it his first headquarters. After the signing of the charter, Prince Rupert, cousin of Charles II, was governor until 1682 when he died.
1670-1	René Cavalier, Sieur de la Salle, reached the Illinois River after having explored the Ohio River in 1669-70.
1671	June 14. Simon François Daumont, Sieur de Saint-Lusson and Father Allovey, a Jesuit, claimed the area around Lake Superior at Sault Ste. Marie.
1672	June 28. Paul Denis de Saint-Simon and Father Albanel claimed the area around James Bay at Fort Charles on the Rupert River.
	Louis de Buade, Comte de Frontenac was appointed governor and served from September 12 until May 9, 1682. He also acted as intendant as well from September 12 until September 16, 1675.
	June 17. Louis Joliet and Father Jacques Marquette discovered the Mississippi River.
1674	October 1. Monseigneur Laval was officially appointed bishop of Quebec.
1682	April 19. La Salle reached the mouth of the Mississippi River, and claimed the land it drained for France.

1683	January 3. His Royal Highness James, Duke of York and brother to Charles II, was elected governor of the Hudson's Bay Company. He resigned when he ascended the throne of England as King James II on February 6, 1685.
1685	April 2. John, Baron Churchill, later first Duke of Marlborough, was elected governor of the Hudson's Bay Company.
	August 1. Jacques René de Brisey, Marquis de Denonville, started his term as governor of New France, which lasted until August 12, 1689.
1686	Pierre, Chevalier de Troyes, supported by the Compagnie du Nord (Compagnie de la Baie d'Hudson), left Montreal overland to Hudson's Bay. He captured Moose Factory, Fort Charles, and Fort Albany. De Troyes returned to Quebec in October and left Pierre le Mayne, Sieur d'Iberville, in charge.
	November 19. The Treaty of Neutrality was signed by England and France. It provided for the creation of a commission to settle boundaries of New France and Rupert's Land. It was agreed that the pre-war boundaries would be returned to until a settlement could be arrived at.
1687	March 1. Louis Alexander des Friches, Chevalier de Menneval, was appointed governor and served until 1690.
1688	January 24. Bishop Laval resigned and died on May 6, 1708 at Quebec.
1689	May 7. William and Mary of England declared war on Louis XIV of France.
	May 31. Governor Denonville was recalled for military service in Europe but was still in New France on August 4, 1689 when the Iroquois renewed hostilities by the Lachine massacre.
	August 12. Louis de Buade, Comte de Frontenac was again appointed governor and died in office on November 28, 1698.

1690   May 20. Des Friches surrendered to New Englanders
        under Sir William Phipps who occupied Port Royal.

1691   April. Captain Joseph Robineau, Sieur de Villebon was
        appointed interim governor of Acadie. He recaptured
        Port Royal on November 27, 1691 and reclaimed Acadie
        for France.

1697   September 20. The Treaty of Ryswick restored Acadie
        officially to France.

1700-1800 STRUGGLE FOR CONTROL

1701   July 24. Detroit was founded by Antoine de la Mathe-
        Cadillac.

        August 4. Peace was concluded at Montreal between the
        French and the Iroquois Confederation.

1705   Spring. St. John's, Newfoundland, was plundered by
        the French, but Fort William was never taken.

1708   December 21-2. Joseph de Saint Ovide de Brouillon cap-
        tured Fort William. He destroyed the fortifications and
        then left.

1710   October 13. Port Royal surrendered to the British,
        under Colonel Francis Nicholson, and was renamed
        Annapolis Royal. This was during the War of the
        Spanish Succession (Queen Anne's War in the Colonies).

1713   April 11. The Peace of Utrecht gave Britain sovereignty
        over Newfoundland including the French post of Placentia,
        the islands of St. Pierre and Miquelon, and the mainland
        of Acadia (Nova Scotia). The French received Ile Saint
        Jean, Ile Royale and all the islands of the St. Lawrence
        River and Gulf. In addition, the French could fish off
        Newfoundland from Cape Bonavista to the northern tip of
        the island and down the western coast to Point Riche. In
        this fishing area, they were allowed to live on land only
        during the fishing season and to erect buildings only for
        drying fish.

1716   William Stewart was sent out to explore the region west
        of Fort York by the Hudson's Bay Company and reached
        the area southeast of Great Slave Lake.

1717   Beginning this year, a series of posts were to be erected
            primarily as bases for exploration westward from Lake
            Superior and secondarily as fur trading posts for the
            French. These posts came to be called the Postes du
            Nord. The first of these was built by Zacharia Robutel
            de la Nöue at Kaministikwia and this became the staging
            area for exploration and further fortifications.

1719   The French began to fortify Louisbourg in Acadia.

1731   First stone fort in the Arctic was started at Fort Prince
            of Wales.

1732   Christophe du Frost, Sieur de la Jemeray built Fort
            Saint Charles on Lake of the Woods.

1738   Fort la Reine (near Portage La Prairie, Manitoba) was
            built by the French.

            October 16. Vérendrye left Fort la Reine and reached a
            Mantanna Indian village (near Spanish, North Dakota) on
            December 3. He left the village on December 13 and re-
            turned to Fort la Reine.

1742   April 29. Vérendrye's sons, Louis-Joseph, Chevalier
            de la Vérendrye and François, Sieur de Tremblay, left
            Fort la Reine to explore the Great Plains. Louis-Joseph
            with some Bow Indians reached the farthest west in the
            vicinity of the Big Horn Mountains in Wyoming on Janu-
            ary 12, 1743. He buried a lead plate at the junction of
            the Bad and Missouri Rivers (Pierre, South Dakota) on
            March 30, 1743. He then met up with his brother and
            they returned to Fort la Reine on July 2.

1744   March 15. France declared war on England beginning the
            War of the Austrian Succession. From August 24 until
            September 25, Annapolis withstood an attack launched
            from Louisbourg by the French.

1749   Louis-Joseph, Chevalier de la Vérendrye, reached the
            fork where the North and South Saskatchewan Rivers join.

            July. Halifax, Nova Scotia, settled and the seat of gov-
            ernment was moved there from Annapolis. Halifax then
            became the commercial center of British North America.

1752   January 1. Marquis Duquesne was appointed governor of New France and served from July 1752 until June 24, 1755.

1753   Louis Chapt, Chevalier de la Corne, built Fort la Corne below the fork of the North and South Saskatchewan Rivers. This post completed a chain of forts which controlled the headwaters of the rivers flowing into Hudson's Bay, thus intercepting Indians on their way to Hudson's Bay Company posts to trade. The French abandoned these posts after the beginning of the French-Indian War which ran from 1756 until 1763.

1754   April 17. Governor Duquesne directed the building of fortifications along the Ohio River and lower Lake Huron. Fort Duquesne, later Pittsburgh, was founded on this date and named after him.

June 26. Anthony Henday left York Fort with some Cree Indians. He reached Moose Lake on the South Saskatchewan River on July 16. The westernmost point reached was near the present site of Calgary on November 21. He then returned to York Fort.

1755   June 21. Fort St. John fell to the British under General Moncton. This was the last French fort in Acadia.

July 28. All Acadians openly sympathetic to the French were ordered deported. The deportation was carried out from September to December 1755 by Captain James Murray and soldiers from New England.

1756   May 17. The French-Indian War in North America, corresponding to the Seven Years War in Europe, started roughly when Great Britain declared war on France.

1758   October 2. A legislative assembly, the first popularly elected parliament in British North America, convened at Halifax with Robert Sanderson as its speaker. The government of Acadia was then in three parts; the governor; the council nominated by the governor and appointed for life by the Crown; and the house of Assembly which was elected by the property owners.

1759   August 17. The governor and council of Acadia divided
                the province into five counties, including Annapolis,
                Kings, Cumberland, Lunenburg and Halifax.

                September 13. Joseph, Marquis de Montcalm, defended
                Quebec against an English assault led by Brevet-Major
                General James Wolfe. Both commanders were killed in
                the struggle but the city eventually fell to the English,
                under General Townshend and Admiral Saunders.

1760   Chesterfield Inlet was discovered by Captain William
                Christopher in the Churchill, sailing from Fort Prince
                of Wales for the English.

                September 8. Governor Vandreuil surrendered Montreal
                to General Jeffrey Amherst, Commander-in-Chief of the
                British forces. Amherst was appointed governor-general
                of British North America and Canada was put under mili-
                tary government. The administration of the country was
                managed by three governments, each reporting to Am-
                herst in New York City. Quebec had been formed on
                September 8, 1759 and governed by Brigadier-General
                James Murray, who had been appointed on October 23,
                1759. After the fall of Montreal, Amherst appointed
                Brigadier-General Thomas Gage to command in Montreal
                and Colonel Ralph Burton to command in Three Rivers,
                both of whom were appointed on September 22, 1760.

1762   June 27. St. John's Newfoundland surrendered to the
                French under Comte d'Haussonville. It was recovered
                by Lord Alexander Colville, however, on September 13
                to 18.

1763   February 10. The Treaty of Paris ended the Seven Years
                War and the French withdrew their competition for the
                fur trade of Rupert's Land and gave up all their claims
                of sovereignty in North America except for the islands of
                St. Pierre and Miquelon, which remain French today.

                October 7. A Royal Proclamation set the boundaries and
                established the government of Quebec. The territory in-
                cluded in the province of Quebec was, roughly, the
                valley of the St. Lawrence River from Nova Scotia on
                the east to Lake Nippissing on the west. Quebec was to
                be ruled by a governor appointed by the Crown, who was

to legislate with the advice of a council and a general
assembly, which he had the power to summon. Also
under this proclamation, St. John's Island (Prince Edward
Island) and Cape Breton Island were annexed to the
government of Nova Scotia, and Labrador to Newfoundland.

1764   July. By a Royal Proclamation the Hudson's Bay Company
was granted free trade with the Indians, subject to limitations imposed by the charter of the company. This
meant that the exclusive trade in Rupert's Land was lawfully reserved to the company and was not subject to further legal action.

August 10. Civil government was re-established in Canada
and General James Murray was appointed governor.

1766   April 7. Major-General Guy Carleton was appointed
lieutenant-governor. He began his term on October 26,
1768 but left for England in 1770 to lobby for changes in
the colonial government of Canada.

1769   June 28. St. John's Island became a separate colony
from Acadia.

1770   August. Captain James Cook, exploring for Great
Britain in the Resolution went through the Bering Strait
on August 11 to Icy Cape, Alaska on August 28, at latitude 71° 17' north, and to North Cape, Siberia on September 1.

December 7. Samuel Hearne, with Matonabee and
Chipewyan Indians, left Fort Prince of Wales. They
reached the mouth of the Coppermine River and started
back on July 18, 1771. On January 9, 1772 Hearne discovered Great Slave Lake and crossed it on his way back
to Fort Prince of Wales.

1771   July 18. Samuel Hearne reached the Arctic Ocean overland via the Coppermine River.

1774   June 22. The Quebec Act was passed by the British Parliament. This Act extended the boundaries of Quebec to
include the land south of Lake Erie to the Ohio River,
west to the Mississippi River, to the Atlantic on the eas
including Labrador, and north to Rupert's Land, which
belonged to the Hudson's Bay Company.

August 7. Juan Pérez in the Santiago sailing for Spain
from Mexico, probably landed at Nootka Sound on Vancouver Island on the West coast.

1775   May 10. During the American Revolution, Ethan Allen
and Benedict Arnold captured Ticonderoga for the Americans. This was followed by the capture of Crown Point
on May 12.

June 9. Governor Carleton proclaimed martial law and
suspended the administrative provisions of the Quebec
Act.

July 14. Bruno Hecata in the Santiago, with Pérez as
co-pilot, landed at Point Grenville, latitude 47° 20'
north, on the Washington coast, claiming the territory
for Spain.

November 13. Richard Montgomery captured Montreal
for the Americans, but failed to take Quebec on December 31 and was killed there.

1776   The term "North West Company" came into use to refer
to a lot of small partnerships of Montreal merchants
that were trading in the area formerly held by the
French forts built in the first half of the century.

July 22. Civil jurisdiction was re-established in the district of Quebec.

1778   May 13. Captain John Meares, sailing in the Felice
Adventurer for the East India Company, arrived at
Nootka Sound and built a house there. He departed in
September.

May 29. Captain James Cook in the Resolution, sailing
for Great Britain, landed at Nootka Sound.

1779   A group of Montreal merchants, commonly known as the
North West Company, formed the North West Society on
a sixteen share basis, held by nine different partnerships of the merchants.

1782   August 8. Fort Prince of Wales was taken by the French,
as was York Fort on August 24. Both forts were destroyed and Fort Prince of Wales was never rebuilt.

1783   September 3. The Treaty of Paris, which ended the American Revolutionary War, defined the United States-Canadian border as running from the mouth of the Pigeon River on Lake Superior, along the Pigeon River, Rainy Lake -Rainy River system to the northwest angle of the Lake of the Woods, then west along latitude 49° north as far as the Mississippi River.

1784   The North West Society was re-organized to become the North West Company.

August 16. New Brunswick was formally separated from Nova Scotia and put under a governor.

August 26. Cape Breton Island was given a separate local government, though it was still under the supervision of the government of Nova Scotia.

September 11. Prince Edward Island was re-annexed to Nova Scotia but retained a separate local government.

1786   April 11. Guy Carleton was appointed governor of all of British North America which gave him control over Quebec, Nova Scotia, Prince Edward Island and Newfoundland.

May 20. Prince Edward Island was again separated from Nova Scotia.

1789   Fort Chipewyan was built on Great Slave Lake and became the headquarters of the North West Company in the Athabaska district. Alexander Mackenzie left there on June 3 and reached the outlet of the Mackenzie River on June 29. He reached the mouth of the river on the Arctic Ocean on July 12, being the first to follow the whole length of the river.

May 6. Estevan José Martinez arrived at Nootka Sound on the west coast in his ship, the <u>Princesa</u>. He had been sent by Revilla-Gigedo, Viceroy of Mexico, to establish Spanish claims in the area.

May 14. Martinez seized Captain William Douglas and the British ship, <u>Iphigenia</u>, but then released them on May 26.

June 24. Martinez took formal possession of Nootka
Port for Spain

July 4. Martinez seized Captain James Colnett, in the
British ship, Argonaut, to prevent him from making a
settlement for Great Britain.

July 14. Martinez seized Captain Hudson and the British
ship, Princess Royal. Both Colnett and Hudson were
sent to San Blas, Mexico where the viceroy released them
and their ships in August.

October 31. Martinez left Nootka Sound.

1790   April 10. Francisco Eliza took possession of Nootka
Port and erected a fort and commanded a garrison
there from 1790 to 1792.

May 31 - August 1. Manuel Quimper, in the Princesa
Real, explored the straits of San Juan de Fuca. He
claimed the area for Spain at Neah Bay on the Olympic
Peninsula on August 1.

October 28. The Nootka Sound Convention was signed
in Madrid, restoring the land and buildings at Nootka
Port, seized by Martinez, to the English. Both countries
agreed to share rights of trade, navigation and settlement of the parts of the coast of North America not already occupied by Spain, and each nation was to have
free access to the establishment of the other country in
this area.

1791   June 19. The Constitutional Act of 1791 was passed in
the British Parliament. This Act established representative government in Canada. While it did not divide
Canada, the Act assumed that a division would take
place between the French speaking area and the English
speaking area, which had been populated by United
Empire Loyalists during and after the American Revolution. The system of government established was to be
headed by a governor who would act with the advice and
consent of a legislative council and two provincial assemblies. The council was to be summoned under the great
seal of the province, and membership was for life. The
governor was empowered to appoint and remove the
speaker of the council. The King was to authorize the

governor to call the assembly once every 12 months.
It could not continue more than four years and the governor could dissolve it at any time.

August 24. By an Order-in-Council, the province of
Quebec was divided into Upper Canada (Ontario) with a
temporary capital at Newark (Niagara-on-the-Lake) and
Lower Canada (Quebec) with its capital at Quebec City.

1792   May 11. Captain Robert Gray, in the American ship,
Columbia, discovered the mouth of the Columbia River.

June 4. Captain George Vancouver explored Puget Sound
and took possession of it for Great Britain at Possession
Sound. He named the area, New Georgia.

July 8. John Graves Simcoe started his term as lieutenant-governor of Upper Canada which lasted until
April 10, 1796.

September 17. Simcoe convened the first legislature of
Upper Canada at Newark.

October 21 - November 10. Lieutenant William Brough-
ton, in the Chatham, navigated the Columbia River up-
stream for one hundred miles and claimed the area for
Great Britain at Point Vancouver.

December 17. The first parliament of Lower Canada
was convened. Jean Antoine Panet was the first speaker.

1793   May 9 - August 24. Alexander Mackenzie, exploring
for the North West Company, started out from Fort-of-
the-Forks, at the Smokey River mouth of the Peace River
and reached the Pacific Ocean at North Bentnick Arm on
July 22. He then returned to Fort-of-the-Forks, being
the first man to reach the Pacific by an overland route
north of Mexico.

May 26 - September 20. Captain George Vancouver ex-
plored the west coast from latitude 56° 30' north to the
Gardner Canal, and New Hanover from the Gardner
Canal to New Georgia, and claimed all the area for
Great Britain.

August 26. Governor Simcoe in Upper Canada established the first permanent capital of the province on the site of an abandoned French fur trading post at Toronto, renaming it York.

1794   France declared war on Great Britain.

1795   The conditions of the Nootka Convention between England and Spain were implemented and Nootka Port vacated by both countries.

1798   The "X Y Company" was organized to compete with the North West Company. Actually the new company was known by several names, including the New North West Company, the X Y Company or Sir Alexander Mackenzie and Company.

The first canal was dug at Sault Ste. Marie by the North West Company on the Canadian side of the rapids.

1799   February 1. St. John's Island, officially called Prince Edward Island after his Royal Highness, Prince Edward, the third son of George III (later the father of Queen Victoria).

August 11. The organization of the Russian-American Company was confirmed by Tsar Paul I. This granted a monopoly of trade on the west coast north of 55° north latitude for twenty years and empowered the company to extend southward into unoccupied territory. The company's main post at Sitka had been established on May 25.

1800-1867   THE FORMING OF THE NATION

1802   March 27. St. Pierre and Miquelon Islands, which had been taken by the British in 1793, were returned to the French by the Treaty of Amiens.

1804   May 14. Two American explorers, Meriweather Lewis and William Clark, left St. Louis. They arrived at the mouth of the Columbia River on November 14, 1805. Here they occupied Fort Clatsop on Young's Bay for the winter and then returned to St. Louis.

1805   Simon Fraser built Rocky Mountin House (Hudson Hope,
            B. C.) as a base for the New Caledonian area. He then
            built Fort St. James on Stuart Lake in 1806 and Fort
            George (Prince George, B. C.) in 1807.

1807   June 30. David Thompson, exploring for the North West
            Company, reached the headwaters of the Columbia
            River. He built Kootenay House at latitude 50° 32' 15"
            north, longitude 115° 51' 40" west. He then left from
            Rocky Mountain House on October 11, 1810 and arrived
            at Tongue Point on July 11, 1811. Thompson was the first
            to follow the Columbia River from its source to the sea.
            At the mouth, he found the men of John Astor's Pacific
            Fur Company, which had been founded on June 23, 1810.
            They had arrived in March and built a post called
            Astoria, in April.

1808   May 28. Simon Fraser left Fort George and followed
            the Fraser River to the sea, arriving at its mouth on
            July 1, 1808. He then returned to Fort George.

1810   February. Rupert's Land was divided into north and
            south administrative areas as part of a re-organization
            of the area called the Wedderburn's Retrenching System.
            The northern department was based in York Territory
            and consisted of York, Churchill, Winnipeg and Saskat-
            chewan districts. The southern department was based
            at Moose Factory and consisted of Moose, Albany and
            Eastmain districts.

            May 31. Wedderburn's Retrenching System was officially
            promulgated by the Hudson's Bay Company. Under this
            system, each trader was to decide his own standard of
            trade, to be outfitted by and responsible to the company,
            and would receive for wages one-half of the profits he
            made. A tract of land in the Red River area was to be
            reserved for retired company servants.

1811   June 13. The control of the Hudson's Bay Company had
            passed to Thomas Douglas, Fifth Earl of Selkirk by
            a stock purchase. He was then granted one hundred and
            sixteen thousand square miles between Lake Winnipeg
            and the headwaters of the Red River. The area, offi-
            cially named Assiniboia, was to be an agricultural
            colony, distinct from but loosely affiliated with the com-
            pany. The area was commonly referred to as the Red
            River Settlement.

1812   June 18. The War of 1812 was declared by the United
                States against Great Britain.

                July. Major-General Isaac Brock, Commander of
                Forces and Acting Administrator, prorogued the
                assembly of Upper Canada and declared martial law.

                August 16. Brock took Detroit from the Americans
                under General William Hull but was later killed at the
                Battle of Queenston Heights on the Niagara River on
                October 13 when repulsing the Americans under General
                Stephen Van Rensselaer.

                August 30. The first settlers sent by Selkirk arrived
                at the Red River Colony and then took formal possession
                on September 4.

1813   July 24. The Battle of Lundy's Lane, the fiercest battle
                of the war, was fought without any gains on either side.
                General Drummond led the British troops, while General
                Brown led the Americans.

                September 13. The Americans, under Captain Oliver
                Perry, defeated the British, under Captain Robert Bar-
                clay, at the naval engagement of Put-in-Bay on Lake Erie.

                October 5. The Americans, under General William
                Harrison, defeated the British, under Colonel Henry
                Proctor, at the Battle of the Thames near Moraviantown.
                Tecumseh, a Shawnee Chief and leader of the Indian
                forces for the British, was killed in this battle. He had
                fought beside General Brock and the two were reputedly
                close friends.

                October 25. The Americans, under General Wade
                Hampton, were defeated on the Chateauguay River by
                French Canadians under Colonel Charles de Salaberry.

                November 30. John McDonald of Garth arrived at the
                mouth of the Columbia River in the British frigate,
                Racoon, under Captain Black. This area had been pur-
                chased from the Pacific Fur Company by the North West
                Company. McDonald formally claimed the area for
                England on December 12. Astoria was renamed Fort
                George.

December 12. Newark (Niagara-on-the Lake, Ontario) was burned by American forces.

December 29. Buffalo was burned by the British.

1814 April 27. York was captured and the Parliament buildings were burned by the Americans. In retaliation, the British landed a small force in New England and burnt the White House in Washington, D. C. and then withdrew. After York was burnt, the seat of government in Upper Canada was moved to Kingston.

September 11. The Americans, under Commodore Thomas MacDonough, defeated the British, under Captain Downie, at the naval battle of Plattsburgh, Lake Champlain.

December 24. The Treaty of Ghent ended the War of 1812. The treaty was ratified by the United States Senate on February 18, 1815. This restored the status quo ante bellum, including the restoration of the area around the mouth of the Columbia River, to the United States.

1815 June 16. The struggle between the North West Company and Lord Selkirk began with the arrest of Miles Macdonell by Duncan Cameran, a North West partner. Cameran then dispersed the colony with the aid of the Métis (French-Indian ancestry) and destroyed the colony's Fort Douglas.

August 13. Lord Selkirk arrived in Canada and hired soldiers to accompany him to the Red River Colony where he captured Fort William. Fort Daer and Fort Douglas were then re-taken from the Métis.

September. Colin Robertson rallied the dispersed Red River colonists together once more and they re-built Fort Douglas.

1816 June 19. The Massacre of Seven Oaks occurred near Fort Douglas. The Métis, under Cuthbert Grant, killed the governor of Rupert's Land, Robert Sample.

A commission of enquiry was appointed by the government to mediate between Selkirk and the North West Company. All the perpetrators were ordered arrested and sent to Montreal to answer for their conduct.

1817   May 1. A Prince Regent's Proclamation put out by the
            Acting Governor of Lower Canada, Sir Gordon Drum-
            mond, required both Selkirk and the North West Company
            to restore all goods seized during the conflict.

1818   October 20. The Convention of 1818 established latitude
            49° north as the United States-Canadian boundary from
            the Lake-of-the-Woods to the Rocky Mountains.

1819   May. Edward Parry, exploring for Great Britain in
            the Hecla and the Griper, left from England. He ex-
            plored Lancaster Sound, Barrow Strait and Melville
            Sound to longitude 110° west. He wintered at Winter
            Harbour, Melville Isle and then returned home.

1820   October 9. Cape Breton Island was reannexed to Nova
            Scotia under a proclamation of lieutenant-governor
            Kempt.

1821   March 21. The Deed Poll was signed and the North West
            Company and the Hudson's Bay Company were united
            under the latter's name. The company was to be run by
            the governor and council of Rupert's Land and the ad-
            ministration was divided into two departments. The
            northern department included Athabaska, Peace, Mac-
            kenzie, New Caledonia and Columbia districts, which
            previously had been outside of the chartered limits of
            Rupert's Land but which were claimed by the North
            West Company by right of exploration and occupancy.
            The southern department comprised the area between
            James Bay and Canada, including the eastern shore of
            Hudson's Bay.

            August 18. John Franklin, sailing for Great Britain,
            reached Point Turnagain, Kent Peninsula, overland from
            York Fort.

1822   Edward Parry discovered Fury and Hecla Straits after
            exploring the east coast of the Melville Peninsula in the
            Arctic.

1824   April. The Russian-American Treaty fixed the boundary
            between their interests on the west coast at latitude 54°
            40' north (Portland Canal) beyond which neither nation
            was to found any establishment without permission of the
            other.

1825   February 28. The Anglo-Russian Treaty relinquished
        Russia's claims from latitude 54° 40' north to longitude
        141° west, then north to the Arctic Ocean. Russia re-
        tained what is now the State of Alaska.

        March 19. Fort Vancouver was founded as the head-
        quarters for the Columbia district.

1827   July 27. Fort Langley, at the head of sea navigation on
        the Fraser River, was settled by Lieutenant A. Emill-
        ius Simpson, Captain of the British ship, Cadbora, and
        Chief Trader, James McMillan, of the Hudson's Bay
        Company.

1829   The Welland Canal was opened to ships between Lake
        Erie and Lake Ontario.

1831   Full control of the whole revenue of the colonies of
        Upper and Lower Canada was granted to the elected
        assemblies.

        June 1. John Ross, exploring for Great Britain in the
        Victory, first described the North Magnetic Pole (dip 89°
        59'; latitude 70° 5' 17" north; longitude 96° 46' 45" west).

1831-2 Lower Fort Garry was built twenty miles downstream
        from the fork of the Red and Assiniboine Rivers.

1832   The Rideau Canal between Bytown (Ottawa) and Kingston
        was completed.

1834   The name of York was changed to Toronto.

1835   Upper Fort Garry was built at the fork of the Red and
        Assiniboine Rivers. This is now the site of Winnipeg,
        Manitoba.

1836   May 4. The Hudson's Bay Company bought back the Red
        River Colony from the Sixth Earl of Selkirk for Ŀ15,000
        worth of the company's stock.

1837   November 6. The Rebellion of 1837 began in Montreal.
        It collapsed on December 13 in St. Eustache and Louis
        Papineau, the chief instigator, fled to the United States.

December 5. The Rebellion of 1837 began in Toronto in Upper Canada. It collapsed there on December 7 when William Lyon Mackenzie, the chief instigator in Upper Canada, fled to the United States.

1838

February 10. The Act to Make Temporary Provision for the Government of Lower Canada was passed. This suspended the constitution of 1791 as of the proclamation of the Act on November 1, 1840. The governor was empowered to set up a special council to make laws which were limited in operation, thus leaving ultimate power with the British colonial office.

May 29. John George Lambton, Earl of Durham, arrived in Canada as governor-in-chief of all British North America, except Newfoundland, and high commissioner for Upper and Lower Canada. His primary mission was to discover the causes of unrest and to make recommendations for providing a more tranquil government in Canada.

November 1. Durham left for England. His report, submitted to the colonial office on February 4, 1839 and laid before the British Parliament on February 11, supplied materials for the legislation concerning Canada between 1839-41 on which modern Canada is founded. He advocated a legislative union between Upper and Lower Canada and prescribed colonial self-government.

1840

July 23. The Act of Union was passed in Britain and became effective for Canada on February 5, 1841. It united the provinces of Upper and Lower Canada, designating them Canada West and East respectively. This Act also provided for an elective assembly and a legislative council appointed for life. A governor-general, appointed by the Crown, was to be the royal representative in the united provinces.

1841

February 10. Kingston was chosen as the capital of Canada.

1842

August 9. The Webster-Ashburton Treaty settled the Maine-New Brunswick boundary.

1843

March 16. Fort Camosun was started by James Douglas of the Hudson's Bay Company. It became known as Fort

Victoria after December 12, following a resolution of the governor and council of the northern department of Rupert's Land.

1844
May 10. The capital of Canada was moved from Kingston to Montreal.

1845
Sir John Franklin explored for Great Britain in the Erelius and the Terror in search of the northwest passage. He left London on May 19 and wintered at Beechey Island in Lancaster Sound. Franklin died on June 11, 1847 and Captain Crozier, the senior officer, abandoned the ships on April 22, 1848. The last record of this expedition was found at Victory Point, dated April 25, 1848. Their fate was unknown until 1859.

June 17. Louis Papineau, former rebel, was elected to head the Canada East Representatives in parliament.

1846
June 15. The Oregon Boundary Treaty set the boundary of Canada and the United States at latitude 49° north from the crest of the Rocky Mountains to the Pacific Ocean. Great Britain got all of Vancouver Island, however.

1847
January 30. James, Eighth Earl of Elgin and Kincardine, was appointed governor-general until December 19, 1854. He allowed the colony of Canada complete self-government in domestic affairs and was the last governor-general with virtual absolute power.

December 6. The assembly in Canada was dissolved by Lord Elgin. The election saw Robert Baldwin of Canada West and Louis LaFontaine of Canada East form a reform ministry on March 11, 1848. This was the first real cabinet in Canada and it marked the beginning of responsible government.

1848
The Tories in Montreal revolted against the proposed Rebellion Losses Bill which would compensate those who had suffered property damage in Lower Canada during the Rebellion of 1837. The parliament buildings were burnt during the disturbances. As a compromise, it was decided to have the assembly meet alternatively in Toronto and Quebec City.

1849   April 25. There were very serious riots in Montreal
                over the Rebellion Losses Bill.

1856   The legislative council (upper house of parliament) was
                made elective in Canada

                May 23. Sir Alan MacNab from Canada West resigned
                from his ministry and was replaced by John Alexander
                MacDonald.

                August 12. Vancouver Island had its first elected
                assembly.

1857   December 28. When gold was discovered in the Couteau
                region of the Fraser and Thompson valleys in 1856 and
                the gold rush began, the need for an official government
                in what is now mainland British Columbia, became
                apparent. James Douglas as lieutenant-governor of Van-
                couver Island, took authority, although legally he had
                no jurisdiction over the area. From December 28, 1857,
                he issued orders concerning the region in the name of
                "Her Majesty's Colonial Government."

1858   August 2. The British parliament passed an Act Provid-
                ing for the Government of the Colony of British Colum-
                bia. The name had been selected by Queen Victoria in
                a letter of July 24. The colony was to include New Cale-
                donia and the Queen Charlotte Islands.

                November 19. Fort Langley was made the capital of
                British Columbia and Douglas took up residence there,
                having been appointed lieutenant-governor of the new
                colony on September 2.

1859   February 14. The capital of British Columbia was moved
                to a place called Queensborough, which then changed
                its name to New Westminster by a Royal Proclamation on
                July 20.

                June. Leopold McClintock discovered the last records
                and fate of the Franklin expedition.

1864   March 30. The Conservative ministry of Sir Etienne
                Taché from Canada East and John A. MacDonald from
                Canada West began. They resigned on June 14 and re-
                organized on June 18 after securing the cooperation of

George Brown and the Liberals by pledging to work for
a federation of Canada East, Canada West, the Maritime Provinces and the North West Territories.

May 11. Dr. Charles Tupper was elected as the Conservative leader of the assembly in Nova Scotia.

September 1. A conference to discuss the uniting of
the Maritime Provinces was called and met in Charlottetown, Prince Edward Island. Canada obtained permission to attend to consider federation of all the provinces. The resulting talks were favorable and another
meeting was called to meet in Quebec City on October
10, 1864.

October 10. The Quebec Conference, with Sir Etienne
Taché as Chairman, passed 72 resolutions as the basis
for further action towards confederation. These were
to be presented to the various provinces for ratification
and to the national parliament of Canada for enactment.
These resolutions formed the basis for the British North
America Act of 1867, the constitution under which Canada
still functions.

1865   The Colonial Laws Validity Act passed by the British
parliament rendered any Canadian legislation, if contrary to legislation of the British parliament, as null and
void.

1866   April 14. Peter Mitchell formed a pro-confederation
ministry in the assembly of New Brunswick. He later
was chosen as a cabinet minister in the first government
of the Dominion of Canada.

August 6. An Act was passed in the British parliament
to unite Vancouver Island with British Columbia. Fred-
rick Seymour became the first governor of the united
colony.

1867-1931   COLONIAL POWER

1867   March 28. The British North America Act became law.

March 30. Alaska became United States' property by
purchase from Russia for $7,200,000.

May 22. An Imperial Order-in-Council declared that the three provinces of Nova Scotia, New Brunswick and Canada (now to be divided into Ontario and Quebec) would be united on July 1 as the Dominion of Canada. The capital was to be at Ottawa.

July 1. John Alexander MacDonald started his tenure as Canada's first Prime Minister.

November. The first parliament of Canada met.

1868   May 25. A Royal Proclamation transferred the capital of British Columbia from New Westminster to Victoria on Vancouver Island.

1869   June 22. The Canadian territorial and administrative control of the North West Territories had its beginnings in the passage by the Parliament of Canada, of an Act for the Temporary Government of Rupert's Land and the North West Territories when united with Canada. Canada paid ₤300,000 and gave large western land grants to the Hudson's Bay Company for the area.

October 11. A federal government survey party under Major Webb was forcibly stopped at St. Vital in Manitoba by André Mault. This was the first open act of rebellion in the Red River area by the Métis.

October 20. A Comité National des Métis de la Riviére Rouge was formed with John Bruce as President and Louis Riel as Secretary.

October 30. Governor-designate, William McDougall, was forbidden to enter the colony at Pembina, Minnesota by the Métis.

November 2. Louis Riel occupied Fort Garry.

November 22. A provisional government was organized by the Métis under the governor and council of the Hudson's Bay Company.

November 30. At night, McDougall slipped across the border at Pembina into Manitoba and read two proclamations laying claim to the area for Canada from December 1. He then slipped back into the United States.

December 8. Riel proclaimed a provisional government to rule until the constitution of full provincial status within the Dominion of Canada could be achieved. This body became known as the First Provisional Government.

December 27. Riel became head of the provisional government after John Bruce resigned.

1870

February 10. The Second Provisional Government was organized, this time including English settlers of the area. Riel continued as President. Commissioners were elected to negotiate with Canada over terms of entry into confederation. Canada wished to give the area territorial status, while Riel wished full provincial status.

March 4. Riel executed Thomas Scott, an Ontario Orangeman. This act subsequently caused a serious rift between French and English Canada.

May 2. By an Act of Parliament, the name of North West Territories was given to the portion of Rupert's Land and the northwestern territories not included in the old district of Assiniboia which was to become a province to be called Manitoba.

June 23. By an Imperial Order-in-Council, Rupert's Land and the other northwestern territories were transferred to Canada, with the capital to be at Fort Garry. Canada officially took over jurisdiction on July 15.

July 15. Manitoba came into the Dominion of Canada as the fifth province.

August 22. Troops under Colonel Garnet Wolseley were despatched by the British Colonial Office and arrived in Red River to publish the proclamation of Canada's claim over the territory. Riel went into exile in the United States.

1870-1

A series of Acts of Parliament were passed by the Canadian government to define the nature of the banking systems in Toronto and Montreal and to make possible further expansion.

1871   May 8. The Treaty of Washington was signed. One of
            the five British representatives was John A. MacDonald.
            This treaty brought about a commerce agreement be-
            tween the United States and Canada.

            June 29. The British North America Act of 1871 con-
            firmed Canada's sovereignty over Rupert's Land and
            the North West territories.

            July 20. British Columbia entered confederation as the
            sixth province. The main condition of entry was that a
            transcontinental railway should be started within two
            years and completed within ten.

1872   Fall. The first Canadian Pacific Railway Company
            collapsed when it was discovered that its President, Sir
            Hugh Allan, had given extensive financial assistance to
            the Conservative Party during the federal election of the
            previous summer.

1873   May 23. An Act of Parliament authorized the establish-
            ment of the North West Mounted Police.

            June 26. By an Imperial Order-in-Council, to be ef-
            fective July 1, Prince Edward Island was admitted into
            confederation as the seventh province. The former
            colony had been embarrassed by debts mainly incurred
            in railroad construction. Canada offered to help in this
            respect.

            November 8. The City of Winnipeg was incorporated.

1874   October. Fort MacLeod (Near Lethbridge, Alta.) was
            begun under the Assistant Commissioner of the North
            West Mounted Police, J. F. MacLeod.

1877   September 22. Treaty No. 7 was signed by Crowfoot,
            Chief of the Blackfoot tribe, at the Blackfoot Crossing of
            the Bow River. This was the last important treaty be-
            tween an Indian tribe and the Canadian Government. It
            ceded to Canada all Indian claims to land north of the
            United States border, east of the Rocky Mountains and
            west of the Cypress Hills.

1880   July 31. An Imperial Order-in-Council annexed all
            British possessions in North America except Newfound-
            land, to Canada. This applied in particular to the Arctic
            Islands, heretofore outside the jurisdiction of any of the
            territories.

1881   February 16. The second Canadian Pacific Railroad
            Company was chartered under George Stephen, Donald
            Smith (later Lord Strathcona), and William Van Horne.

1882   May 8. An Order-in-Council created four provisional
            districts of Athabaska, Assiniboia, Alberta and Saskat-
            chewan with the capital at Regina.

            December 6. The North West Mounted Police moved
            their headquarters to Regina.

1884   Sir Charles Tupper, the Canadian High Commissioner
            in London, was associated with Sir Robert Morier, the
            British Ambassador to Spain, in an unsuccessful
            attempt to negotiate a trade treaty between Spain and
            England.

1885   March 18. Riel led a second rebellion of Indians and
            Métis in Saskatchewan. On March 19, Riel set up a
            provisional government at Batoche with Pierre Parenteau
            as president and Gabriel Dumont as adjutant-general.
            The North West Mounted Police, under Superintendent
            L. Crozier, were defeated by Dumont at Duck Lake on
            March 26. The rebellion collapsed when government
            militia under General Middleton captured Batoche on
            May 12 and when Riel surrendered on May 15. Big Bear
            and his Cree Indians surrendered to Major-General T.B.
            Strange near Fort Carlton on July 2. Riel was hanged on
            November 16 after a trial at Edmonton, Alberta. The
            hanging of Riel served to further the rift between Protes-
            tant English Ontario and Catholic French Quebec.

            November 7. The Canadian Pacific Railroad was com-
            pleted at Craigellachie, British Columbia.

1886   The Trades and Labor Congress of Canada was organ-
            ized.

1888   July 12. The Jesuit Estates Act was passed in Quebec.
            This provided financial compensation to the Jesuit order
            for lands which had reverted to the Crown when the order
            had ceased to exist for a time. The passage of this Act
            was not welcomed in English Canada.

1890   March 31. The Manitoba Schools Act (provincial) intro-
            duced an exclusive non-denominational English system
            of education in the province. The French in Manitoba

and Quebec fought this and the question was finally
settled by the Canadian Prime Minister, Laurier, by
insuring that there would be teachers in the French
areas who could speak French and that religion could be
taught after formal school hours if desired by the Catho-
lics. In 1912-16, there was a similar problem in Ontario.

1891   June 6. Sir John A. MacDonald, Canada's first Prime
            Minister, died.

1893   Sir Charles Tupper, the Canadian High Commissioner
            in London, and Lord Dufferin, the British Ambassador
            to France, negotiated a commercial treaty between
            Great Britain and France regulating the customs tariff
            in commercial relations between France and Canada.
            Both Tupper and Dufferin signed the treaty.

1896   August 16. Gold was discovered on Bonanza Creek in
            the Klondike by George Cormack and two Indians,
            Skookum Jim and Tagish Charlie.

1897   August 16. An Order-in-Council created the District
            of the Yukon as a separate judicial district to be admin-
            istered by a commission of six men.

1898   June 13. The Yukon was made a separate territory with
            its capital at Dawson City. In April of 1953, the capital
            was moved to Whitehorse.

1899   October. A contingent of volunteers were sent out to
            South Africa to fight in the "Boer War." In all, 7,000
            Canadians served there. The conflict ended in 1902.

1900   June 8. The White Pass and Yukon Railway was com-
            pleted at Careross, connecting Skagway, Alaska and
            Whitehorse in the Yukon.

1901   December 12. Marconi received the first trans-Atlantic
            radio signal at Cabot Tower, St. John's Newfoundland.
            This proved that radio signals reached beyond the hori-
            zon and thus was a considerable breakthrough in com-
            munications.

1902   The Canadian and Catholic Confederation of Labor was
            established by some French Canadian unions.

1903   The Alaska-British Columbia boundary was settled by a joint British-American tribunal of 3 Americans, 2 Canadians and Lord Alverstone, the British representative. The vote found in favor of the American claim by 4-2 and created dissatisfaction in Canada (both Canadians had voted negatively, while Alverstone voted with the Americans).

June 16. Roald Amundsen led a Norwegian expedition in the Gjoa through the North West Passage. They were the first to navigate the passage, leaving in June and returning home on August 31, 1906.

June 19. Regina was incorporated as a city.

July 21. Saskatoon was incorporated as a city.

1905   July 25. The North West Territories Act set new boundaries to the territories to exclude the province of Manitoba and the forthcoming provinces of Alberta and Saskatchewan.

September 1. Alberta and Saskatchewan entered confederation as the eighth and ninth provinces.

1909   The Boundary Waters Treaty established an International Joint Committee to settle disputes between the United States and Canada. The committee consisted of 3 Americans and 3 Canadians.

February 23. The first heavier-than-air flight in British Empire took place at Badek, Nova Scotia. J.A.D. McCurdy was the pilot.

April 6. Commander Peary reached the North Pole. His ship had been commanded by Captain Bartlett of Newfoundland.

1910   The Naval Bill was proposed by Prime Minister Laurier to create a small Canadian navy. This was opposed by the French and the bill never passed.

1912   Prime Minister Borden introduced the New Naval Bill which was passed and created a Canadian Navy.

1914	August 4. Great Britain declared war on Germany and Canada was automatically at war also. 424,859 Canadians served overseas and 60,661 were killed or missing during the conflict.
1917	The first federal income tax law was passed. This form of taxation had existed provincially since 1876.
	June. The Military Service Act was introduced by Prime Minister Borden. It passed, but created a split in the majority Liberal Party along French-English lines. The result was a coalition led by Borden, called the Union Government, which won a bitter election on the issue of conscription in December.
	December 8. An explosion aboard a French munitions ship in Halifax harbor wiped out half of that city.
1918	March and April. There were serious riots against conscription in Quebec City.
1919	April 28. The League of Nations was founded, and Canada signed the charter.
	May 15. The only general strike in Canadian history occurred when 30,000 workers in Winnipeg went out. This was the result of an effort to organize the One Big Union (OBU). On June 17, the leaders of the strike were arrested. On June 21, police and troops intervened to suppress a "riot" and by June 25, the strike had collapsed. The leaders were eventually jailed.
	June 14. Sir John Alcock and Sir Arthur Brown left from Newfoundland to try and cross the Atlantic non-stop by plane. They landed in Ireland the next day to claim a prize of £10,000 offered by the London Daily Mail for the task. The flight took 15 hours and 57 minutes.
	June 28. The Versailles Peace Treaty was signed, ending the first World War.
1921	Prime Minister A. Meighen took a very independent line against the Anglo-Japanese Treaty and persuaded the British not to renew it at the Imperial Conference that year.

1922   September. During the Chanak crisis, Prime Minister Mackenzie King made it clear that Canada would not automatically undertake to support British commitments in Europe. He also declared that Canada did not consider herself bound by the resulting Treaty of Lausanne which was reached between Great Britain and Turkey on July 24, 1923.

1923   Ernest Lapointe signed the Halibut Treaty with the United States as the sole representative of the King.

Sir Frederick Banting was awarded the Nobel Prize for the discovery of insulin with Dr. Charles Best.

February 2. The Grand Trunk Railway was taken over by the government.

1926   The Balfour Declaration gave British recognition of the autonomy of the Dominions.

May 9. The North Pole was first flown over by Richard E. Byrd.

1927   The All-Canadian Congress of Labor was formed.

1931-1973   AUTONOMY

1931   December 11. The Statute of Westminster became law. This fulfilled the recommendations of the Balfour report and made the necessary legal changes to effect the Dominions' new position of equality with England.

1932   Prime Minister R. B. Bennett set up the Canadian Broadcasting Commission to control broadcasting.

1933   July. The Regina Manifesto was issued by the Co-Operative Commonwealth Federation (CCF).

1934   The Bank of Canada was established to control banks in Canada.

1935   The Canada Wheat Board Act set up a board of grain commissioners to control sales of wheat in order to solve some of the problems of the depression.

Appeals from Canadian courts to the Judicial Committee of the Privy Council in England were abolished in criminal cases.

Appeals in civil cases were abolished in 1949.

1937   The Sirois Commission was appointed to settle disputes between the dominion and the provinces over legislative powers.

1939   September 10. Canada entered the Second World War a week after Britain had declared war.

1940   Canada made an agreement with the United States on defense of North America. The talks were held at Ogdensburg.

The Rowell-Sirois Commission on federal and provincial affairs, presented its report to the government.

The Canadian Congress of Labour formed out of the old All-Canadian Congress of Labour and unions associated with the American Congress of Industrial Organizations.

June 23. The Royal Canadian Mounted Police ship, St. Roche, began the west-east voyage through the North West Passage. She completed the journey on October 11, 1942 and then travelled back through the passage from west to east, completing the trip on October 16, 1944. She was the first ship to make the voyage both ways.

July 10. The British North American Act was amended to provide for the Unemployment Insurance Act.

1941   April 20. The Hyde Park Agreement was reached. This tied the United States and Canadian economies closer together by the heavy purchasing of Canadian war material by the United States and a plan for shared defense costs.

1942   February 26. Japanese-Canadians ordered to be moved inland from Pacific Coast, which was one of the last acts of open and legal discrimination on the part of the government. Some compensation was paid after the war and there were numerous court cases which resulted in further compensation.

April 27. A national plebiscite on conscription was held. It passed, though Quebec voted solidly, "No." No conscripts were sent overseas, however, until November 1944. At this time, there were riots in Montreal, but the crisis ended with the war and conscription has never been reintroduced.

November 20. The Alcan Highway was officially opened at Mile 1061, near Soldier Summit. This highway runs from Dawson Creek, British Columbia to Fairbanks, Alaska.

1943   August 10. The sixth Anglo-American War Conference between Churchill and Roosevelt opened at Quebec City. The conference ended on August 24.

1944   June 6. Canadian troops landed with the Allies in Europe as part of D-Day.

September 11. The second conference between Churchill and Roosevelt was held at Quebec City. This conference closed on September 16.

1945   February 20. The first family allowance cheques were mailed in Canada.

May 8. This was V-E Day, which saw the end to fighting in Europe. The war had cost 41,700 Canadian lives.

June 26. The United Nations charter was signed in San Francisco.

August 15. The conflict in the Pacific ended on V-J Day with the defeat of Japan. On September 2, the Japanese forces were surrendered on the U.S. battleship, Missouri.

1946   February 5. A Royal Commission was appointed to investigate Russian expionage activity in Canada which had been disclosed by Igor Gouzenko who had defected from the Soviet Embassy in Ottawa in September 1945.

July 20. The Paris Peace Conference began.

1949   The Massey Commission was established to investigate the state of the Canadian culture.

April 1. Newfoundland entered confederation as the tenth province. A referendum had been held in July 1948 and the terms of union had been signed by provincial and federal authorities in December 1948.

April 3. The North Atlantic Treaty was signed at Washington, D.C.

December 16. An amendment was made to the British North America Act. This empowered the Canadian parliament to amend the constitution in matters affecting the federal government only. After 1949, the only important limitation on Canada's autonomy was the function of the British parliament to amend the British North America Act in matters affecting both the Dominion and the provinces.

1950   The Columbo Plan of aid to developing nations was adopted by the British Commonwealth of Nations.

June 26. North Korean forces invaded South Korea. Canada participated in the Koren war by maintaining a brigade in the Commonwealth Division.

1951   The Massey Royal Commission on the Arts, Letters and Sciences submitted its report to the government. This led to the establishment of the Canada Council in 1957 which gives financial encouragement in many fields.

May 31. An amendment to the British North America Act provided for the Old Age Security Act.

September 3. The Pacific Security Pact was signed.

1952   January 25. Vincent Massey was appointed the first Canadian Governor-General of Canada.

September 6. The Canadian Broadcasting Corporation began television transmission in Montreal. This was followed on September 8 with the first transmission in Toronto. By 1958, a micro-wave system had been completed from coast-to-coast.

1953	July 29. The Korean armistice was signed.
1954	Canada was chosen to supervise the Indo-China armistice, along with Poland and India.
1956	September 25. The trans-Atlantic telephone cables between Britain and North America were inaugurated.

1956 · October. The Canadian Secretary of State for External Affairs, L. B. Pearson, was largely responsible for the despatch of the United Nations Emergency Forces to Egypt in opposition to Britain and France. He subsequently was awarded the Nobel Peace Prize for 1957.

1958 · The North American Defense Organization was begun (NORAD).

1959 · The Distant Early Warning Line (DEW Line) was established in a cooperative defense effort between the United States and Canada.

April 25. The first sea-going vessels entered the St. Lawrence Seaway.

June 26. President Eisenhower of the United States and Queen Elizabeth opened the St. Lawrence Seaway at St. Lambert Lock in Montreal.

1960 · A Canadian contingent was despatched with the United Nations Emergency Forces to the Congo.

August 10. The Canadian Bill of Rights was given Royal assent.

1961 · Summer. The New Democratic Party was formed out of a CCF trade union alliance.

1962 · A Canadian-built satellite, "Alouette," was launched to study the ionosphere. In 1965 and 1967, others were launched, all of which were extremely successful.

September 3. The trans-Canada highway was officially opened.

December 11. The last hangings in Canada occurred when R. Turpin (killed a policeman) and A. Lucas (killed a Detroit narcotics agent) were executed in Toronto.

1963	The Royal Commission on Bilingualism and Biculturalism was appointed.

The Columbia River Treaty was ratified.

1964	A Canadian contingent was despatched with the United Nations Emergency Forces to Cyprus.

1965	February 15. The Canadian "maple leaf" flag was proclaimed as the official flag of Canada to replace the old red ensign. Over the period from 1965 to 1967, the unification of the separate military forces in Canada took place under the name of the Canadian Armed Forces.

1966	May 18. Paul Joseph Chartler of Toronto was killed by his own bomb when it blew up prematurely in a washroom in the Houses of Parliament in Ottawa. He had intended to throw it into the Commons chamber. This is the only incidence of such violence against parliament in Canadian history.

1967	April 27. The World's Fair, more commonly known as Expo 67, was opened in Montreal.

July 1. Canada celebrated its centenary.

November 7. The continental shelf was declared to be under federal and not provincial jurisdiction by a ruling of the Supreme Court of Canada.

1969	January 22. Ottawa announced its intent to discuss exchange of ambassadors with Communist China.

September 14. The United States oil tanker, Manhattan, became the first commercial ship to voyage through the North West Passage.

October 15. Canada and the Vatican established diplomatic relations.

1970	October 5. James Cross, the British Trade Commissioner to Canada, was kidnapped by a cell of the Front de Liberation Quebecois (FLQ). Cross was subsequently released and 3 of the kidnappers were flown to Cuba on December 3.

October 17. The body of Pierre Laporte, the Quebec Minister of Labour, was found. Laporte had been kidnapped on October 10 by another cell of the FLQ. Four men were subsequently detained and charged with his murder.

December 2. The Canadian government invoked the War Measures Act which suspended many civil liberties, including habeas corpus. This Act was allowed to lapse on April 30, 1971, after the FLQ terrorism in Quebec was seen to have subsided.

1971 January 4. Paul Rose, Jacques Rose, Francis Simard, and Bernard Lortie, were convicted as being criminally responsible for the death of Pierre Laporte.

March 31. Paul Rose was sentenced to life imprisonment for the non-capital murder of Laporte. On November 30 he was sentenced to life for kidnapping as well. On May 20, Francis Simard was sentenced to life for murder, and on November 22, Bernard Lortie was sentenced to 20 years for kidnapping.

March 22. Nova Scotia became the first province to allow television cameras into its legislature on a regular basis.

April 30. The anti-terrorist Public Order (War Measures) Act was allowed to lapse by the federal government.

August 4. An agreement was announced in Moscow for the establishment of a Canadian-Soviet working group on Artic scientific research.

October 20. Soviet Premier Kosygin and Prime Minister Trudeau signed an agreement at Ottawa providing for more expanded exchanges between Canada and the USSR in scientific, technical, and cultural fields.

1972 May 6. Abraham Okpik, the first Eskimo member of the Northwest Territories legislative council, completed a two-year, 45,000 mile journey through the territories to help 13,000 Eskimos select new names. Until this time, Eskimos had had only one name, which they frequently changed. This created numerous problems for the government and in 1945 each Eskimo was issued a number to be worn around his neck from birth. On all legal documents

the number as well as the name was recorded but this practice was considered too impersonal and in 1970 Okpik was
selected by the Eskimos and the government to record the
names of the Eskimo population.

October 30. The federal election reduced Prime Minister
Trudeau and the Liberal Party to a minority government.
The combined opposition parties had more votes than the
government in Parliament. A minority government can
only last so long as it can persuade enough M.P.'s from
the opposition parties to give it a majority in votes on bills,
etc.

December 27. Former Prime Minister and the winner of
the Nobel Peace Prize in 1957, Lester B. Pearson, died at
his home in Ottawa at the age of 75.

1973   April 20. A Canadian communications satellite, Anik II,
was launched from Cape Kennedy, U.S.A. to function as
a backup to Anik I, launched on November 9, 1972. The
two satellites will provide radio and television to communities north of the arctic circle which had previously only
been served by short-wave radio. Surplus channels on
Anik II have been rented by several American companies
for communication purposes.

Prime Ministers of Canada

Sir John A. Macdonald	cons.	July 1, 1867-November 5, 1873
Alexander Mackenzie	lib.	November 7, 1873-October 16, 1878
Sir John A. Macdonald	cons.	October 17, 1878-June 6, 1891
Sir John Abbott	cons.	June 16, 1891-November 24, 1892
Sir John Thompson	cons.	December 5, 1892-December 12, 1894
Sir Mackenzie Bowell	cons.	December 21, 1894-April 27, 1896
Sir Charles Tupper	cons.	May 1, 1896-July 8, 1896
Sir Wilfred Laurier	lib.	July 11, 1896-October 6, 1911
Sir Robert L. Borden	cons.	October 10, 1911-July 10, 1920
Arthur Meighen	cons.	July 10, 1920-December 29, 1921
W. L. Mackenzie King	lib.	December 29, 1921-June 28, 1926
Arthur Meighen	cons.	June 29, 1926-September 25, 1926
W, L. Mackenzie King	lib.	September 25, 1926-August 6, 1930
Richard B. Bennett	cons.	August 7, 1930-October 23, 1935
W.L. Mackenzie King	lib.	October 23, 1935-November 15, 1948
Louis St. Laurent	lib.	November 15, 1948-June 21, 1957
John G. Diefenbaker	cons.	June 21, 1957-April 22, 1963
Lester B. Pearson	lib.	April 23, 1963-April 20, 1968
Pierre E. Trudeau	lib.	April 20, 1968 -

Premiers of Ontario

John S. Macdonald	cons.	July 16, 1867-December 20, 1871
Edward Blake	lib.	December 20, 1871-October 25, 1872
Oliver Mowat	lib.	October 25, 1872-July 25, 1896
A. S. Hardy	lib.	July 25, 1896-October 21, 1899
G. W. Ross	lib.	October 21, 1899-February 8, 1905
Sir. J. P. Whitney	cons.	February 8, 1905-October 2, 1914
Sir William Hearst	cons.	October 2, 1914-November 14, 1919
E. G. Drury	united farmers	November 14, 1919-July 16, 1923
G. H. Ferguson	cons.	July 16, 1923-December 15, 1930
G. S. Henry	cons.	December 15, 1930-July 10, 1934
M. F. Hepburn	lib.	July 10, 1934-October 21, 1942
G. D. Conant	lib.	October 21, 1942-May 18, 1943
H. C. Nixon	lib.	May 18, 1943-August 17, 1943
Goerge Drew	cons.	August 17, 1943-October 19, 1948
T. L. Kennedy	cons.	October 19, 1948-May 4, 1949
Leslie M. Frost	cons.	May 4, 1949-November 8, 1961
John P. Robarts	cons.	November 8, 1961-March, 1971
William Davis	cons.	March, 1971

Premiers of Quebec

Pierre J. C. Chauveau	cons.	July 15, 1867-February 27, 1873
Gedeon Ouimet	cons.	February 27, 1873-September 22, 1874
Charles Boucher	cons.	September 22, 1874-March 8, 1878
Henri Joly	lib.	March 8, 1878-October 31, 1879
Joseph-Adolphe Chapleau	cons.	October 31, 1879-August 1, 1882
J.-Alfred Mousseau	cons.	August 1, 1882-January 23, 1884
John J. Ross	cons.	January 23, 1884-January 13, 1887
L. -Olivier Taillon	cons.	January 13, 1887-January 29, 1887
Honore Mercier	lib.	January 29, 1887-December 21, 1891
Charles Boucher	cons.	December 21, 1891-December 16, 1892
L. -Olivier Taillon	cons.	December 16, 1892-May 11, 1896
Edmund J. Flynn	cons.	May 11, 1896-May 24, 1897
F. -Gabriel Marchand	lib.	May 24, 1897-October 3, 1900
S. -Napoleon Parent	lib.	October 3, 1900-March 23, 1905
Sir Lomer Gouin	lib.	March 23, 1905-July 9, 1920
L.-Alexandre Taschereau	lib.	July 9, 1920-June 11, 1936
Adelard Godbout	lib.	June 11, 1936-August 24, 1936
Maurice Duplessis	union nat.	August 24, 1936-November 8, 1939
Adelard Godbout	lib.	November 8, 1939-August 30, 1944
Maurice Duplessis	union nat.	August 30, 1944-September 10, 1959
Jean-Paul Sauve	union nat.	September 10, 1959-January 7, 1960
Antonio Barrette	union nat.	January 7, 1960-July 5, 1960
Jean Lesage	lib.	July 5, 1960-June 16, 1966
Daniel Johnson	union nat.	June 16, 1966-April 29, 1970
Robert Bourassa	lib.	April 29, 1970 -

Premiers of New Brunswick

A. R. Wetmore	cons.	1867-1872
G. E. King	lib.	1872-1878
J. J. Fraser	cons.	1878-1882
D. L. Hannington	cons.	1882-1883
A. G. Blair	lib.	1883-1896
James Mitchell	cons.	1896-October 29, 1897
H. R. Emerson	lib.	October 29, 1897-August 31, 1900
L. J. Tweedie	cons.	August 31, 1900-March 6, 1907
William Pugsley	lib.	March 6, 1907-May 31, 1907
C. W. Robinson	lib.	May 31, 1907-March 24, 1908
J. D. Hazen	cons.	March 24, 1908-October 16, 1911
James K. Flemming	cons.	October 16, 1911-December 17, 1914
George G. Clarke	cons.	December 17, 1914-February 1, 1917
James Murray	cons.	February 1, 1917-April 4, 1917
Walter E. Foster	lib.	April 4, 1917-February 28, 1923
Peter Veniot	lib.	February 28, 1923-September 14, 1925
John Baxter	cons.	September 14, 1925-May 19, 1931
Charles D. Richards	cons.	May 19, 1931-June 1, 1933

L. P. D. Tilley	cons.	June 1, 1933-July 16, 1935
A. Allison Dysart	lib.	July 16, 1935-March 13, 1940
J. B. McNair	lib.	March 13, 1940-October 8, 1952
H. J. Fleming ,	cons.	October 8, 1952-July 12, 1960
Louis J. Robichand	lib.	July 12, 1960-October 26, 1970
Richard Hatfield	cons.	October 26, 1970 -

Premiers of Nova Scotia

H. Blanchard	cons.	July 4, 1867-November 7, 1867
William Annand	lib.	November 7, 1867-May 11, 1875
P. C. Hill	lib.	May 11, 1875-October 22, 1878
S. H. Holmes	cons.	October 22, 1878-May 25, 1882
J. S. D. Thompson	cons.	May 25, 1882-August 3, 1882
W. T. Pipes	lib.	August 3, 1882-July 28, 1884
W. S. Fielding	lib.	July 28, 1884-July 20, 1896
George H. Murray	lib.	July 20, 1896-January 24, 1923
E. H. Armstrong	lib.	January 24, 1923-July 16, 1925
E. N. Rhodes	cons.	July 16, 1925-August 11, 1930
Col. Gordon Harrington	cons.	August 11, 1930-September 5, 1933
Angus Macdonald	lib.	September 5, 1933-July 10, 1940
A. S. MacMillan	lib.	July 10, 1940-September 8, 1945
Angus L. Macdonald	lib.	September 8, 1945-April 13, 1954
Harold Connolly	lib.	April 13, 1954-September 30, 1954
Henry D. Hicks	lib.	September 30, 1954-November 20, 1956
Robert L. Stanfield	cons.	November 20, 1956-September 13, 1967
George I. Smith	cons.	September 13, 1967-October 13, 1970
Gerald A. Regan	lib.	October 13, 1970 -

Premiers of Manitoba

A. Boyd	cons.	September 16, 1870-December 14, 1871
N. A. Girard	cons.	December 14, 1871-March 14, 1872
J. H. Clarke	cons.	March 14, 1872-July 8, 1874
N. A. Girard	cons.	July 8, 1874-December 3, 1874
R. A. Davis	cons.	December 3, 1874-October 16, 1878
John Norquay	cons.	October 16, 1878-December 26, 1887
D. H. Harrison	cons.	December 26, 1887-January 19, 1888
T. Greenway	lib.	January 19, 1888-January 8, 1900
H. J. Macdonald	cons.	January 8, 1900-October 29, 1900
Sir R. P. Robin	cons.	October 29, 1900-May 12, 1915
T. C. Norris	cons.	May 12, 1915-August 8, 1922
John Bracken	coalition	August 8, 1922-January 8, 1943
S. S. Garson	coalition	January 8, 1943-November 7, 1948
D. L. Campbell	lib.	November 7, 1948-June 16, 1958
Dufferin Roblin	cons.	June 16, 1958-November 27, 1967
Walter Weir	cons.	November 27, 1967-June 25, 1969
Edward Schreyer	n.d.p.	June 25, 1969 -

Premiers of British Columbia

J. F. McCreight	----	November 13, 1871-December 23,1872
Amor DeCosmos	----	December 23, 1872-February 11, 1874
G. A. Walkem	----	February 11, 1874-February 1, 1876
A. C. Elliot	----	February 1, 1876-June 25, 1878
G. A. Walkem	----	June 25, 1878-June 13, 1882
R. Beaver	----	June 13, 1882-January 29, 1883
William Smythe	----	January 29, 1883-May 15, 1887
A. E. B. Davie	----	May 15, 1887-August 2, 1889
J. Robson	----	August 2, 1889-July 2, 1892
T. Davie	----	July 2, 1892-March 4, 1895
J. H. Turner	----	March 4, 1895-Agust 12, 1898
C. A. Semlin	----	August 12, 1898-February 28, 1900
Joseph Martin	----	February 28, 1900-June 15, 1900
James Dunsmuir	----	June 15, 1900-November 21, 1902
E. G. Prior	----	November 21, 1902-June 1, 1903
Richard McBride	cons.	June 1, 1903-December 15, 1915
William J. Bowser	cons.	December 15, 1915-November 23,191
Harlan Brewster	lib.	November 23, 1916-March 6, 1918
John Olicer	lib.	March 6, 1918-August 20, 1927
John D. Maclean	lib.	August 20, 1927-August 21, 1928
Simon Tolmie	cons.	August 21, 1928-November 15, 1933
T. D. Pattullo	lib.	November 15, 1933-December 9, 194
John Hart	coalition	December 9, 1941-January 18, 1947
Byron Johnson	coalition	January 18, 1947-August 1, 1952
W. A. C. Bennett	social credit	August 1, 1952-August 30, 1972
David Barrett	n.d.p.	August 30, 1972-

Premiers of Prince Edward Island

James C. Pope	cons.	April, 1873-September, 1873
L. C. Owen	cons.	September, 1873- August, 1876
L. H. Davies	cons.	August, 1876-April 25, 1879'
W. W. Sullivan	cons.	April 25, 1879-November, 1889
N. McLeod	cons.	November, 1889-April 27, 1891
F. Peters	lib.	April 27, 1891-October, 1897
A. B. Warburton	lib.	October, 1897- August, 1898
D. Farquharson	lib.	August, 1898-December 29, 1901
A. Peters	lib.	December 29, 1901-Februaryl, 1908
F. L Haszard	lib.	February 1, 1908-May 16, 1911
H. James Palmer	lib.	May 16, 1911-December 2, 1911
John Mathieson	cons.	December 2, 1911-June 21, 1917
Aubin Arsenault	cons.	June 21, 1917-September 9, 1919
J. H. Bell	lib.	September 9, 1919-September 5, 192
James D. Stewart	cons.	September 5, 1923-August 12, 1927
Albert C. Saunders	lib.	August 12, 1927-May 20, 1930
Walter M. Lea	lib.	May 20, 1930-August 29, 1931

James D. Stewart	cons.	August 29, 1931-October 14, 1933
William MacMillan	cons.	October 14, 1933-August 15, 1935
Walter M. Lea	lib.	August 15, 1935-January 14, 1936
Thane A. Campbell	lib.	January 14, 1936-May 11, 1943
J. Walter Jones	lib.	May 11, 1943-May 25, 1953
A. W. Matheson	lib.	May 25, 1953-September 1, 1959
Walter R. Shaw	cons.	September 1, 1959- May 11, 1970
A. B. Campbell	lib.	May 11, 1970 -

Premiers of Alberta

Alex Rutherford	lib.	September 2, 1905-May 26, 1910
A. L. Sifton	lib.	May 26, 1910-October 30, 1917
Charles Stewart	lib.	October 30, 1917-August 13, 1921
Herbert Greenfield	united farm.	August 13, 1921-November, 1925
John E. Brownlee	united farm.	November, 1925-July 10, 1934
Richard G. Reid	united farm.	July 10, 1934-September 3, 1935
William Aberhart	soc. credit	September 3, 1935-May 31, 1943
E. C. Manning	soc. credit	May 31, 1943-December 12, 1968
H. E. Strom	soc. credit	December 12, 1968-August 30, 1971
Peter Lougheed	cons.	August 30, 1971 -

Premiers of Saskatchewan

Walter Scott	lib.	September 12, 1905-October 20, 1916
W. M. Martin	lib.	October 20, 1916-April 5, 1922
C. A. Dunning	lib.	April 5, 1922-February 26, 1926
J. G. Gardiner	lib.	February 26, 1926-September 9, 1929
J. T. M. Anderson	cons.	September 9, 1929-July 19, 1934
J. G. Gardiner	lib.	July 19, 1934-November 1, 1935
W. J. Patterson	lib.	November 1, 1935-July 10, 1944
T. C. Douglas	c.c.f.	July 10, 1944-November 7, 1961
W. S. Lloyd	c.c.f.	November 7, 1961-May 22, 1964
W. R. Thatcher	lib.	May 22, 1964-June 23, 1971
Alan Blackeney	n.d.p.	June 23, 1971 -

Premiers of Newfoundland

| Joseph Smallwood | lib. | April 1, 1949-October 28, 1971 |
| Frank Moore | cons. | October 28, 1971 |

Abbreviations

lib. -- Liberal Party
cons. -- Conservative Party and later the Progressive Conservative Party
c.c.f. -- Cooperative Commonwealth Federation
n.d.p. -- New Democratic Party (former c.c.f.)
soc. credit -- Social Credit Party
union nat. -- Union Nationale Party
united afrm. -- United Farmers Party

PRE-1867 CONSTITUTIONAL DOCUMENTS

Introduction

The three most important steps towards the limited self-determination granted by the British North America Act of 1867 were the Quebec Act of 1774, the Constitutional Act of 1791, and the Act of Union of 1840. These three statutes represent the British Parliament's efforts to adapt its governance of the territory to the changing needs of a multi-racial population and the unique difficulties of the growing country.

The texts of the three Acts are based upon the original printed editions as authorized by the British Parliament to be done by the King's Printer of the period. Short titles have been omitted but otherwise the texts have been reproduced in their entirety.

THE QUEBEC ACT

ANNO DECIMO QUARTO

GEORGII III. REGIS.

CAP. LXXXIII.

An Act for making more effectual Provision for the
Government of the Province of Quebec in North America.

Whereas His Majesty, by His Royal Proclamation, bearing Date the
Seventh Day of October, in the Third Year of His Reign, thought fit to declare the Provisions which had been made in respect to certain Countries,
Territories, and Islands in America, ceded to His Majesty by the defini-
tive Treaty of Peace, concluded at Paris on the Tenth Day of February, One
Thousand seven hundred and sixty-three: And whereas, by the Arrange-
ments made by the said Royal Proclamation, a very large Extent of Country, within which there were several Colonies and Settlements of the Subjects of France, who claimed to remain therein under the Faith of the said
Treaty, was left, without any Provision being made for the Administration
of Civil Government therein; and certain Parts of the Territory of Canada,
where sedentary Fisheries had been established and carried on by the Subjects of France, Inhabitants of the said Province of Canada, under Grants
and Concessions from the Government thereof, were annexed to the Government of Newfoundland, and thereby subjected to Regulations inconsistent
with the Nature of such Fisheries: May it therefore please Your most Excellent Majesty that it may be enacted; and be it enacted by the King's most
Excellent Majesty, by and with the Advice and Consent of the Lords Spiritual
and Temporal and Commons, in this present Parliament assembled, and
by the Authority of the same, That all the Territories, Islands, and Countries in North America, belonging to the Crown of Great Britain, bounded
on the South by a Line from the Bay of Chaleurs, along the High Lands which
divide the Rivers that empty themselves into the River Saint Lawrence from
those which fall into the Sea, to a Point in Forty-five Degrees of Northern
Latitude, on the Eastern Bank of the River Connecticut, keeping the same
Latitude directly West, through the Lake Champlain, until, in the same
Latitude, it meets the River Saint Lawrence; from thence up the Eastern
Bank of the Said River to the Lake Ontario; thence through the Lake Ontario,
and the River commonly called Niagara; and thence along by the Eastern
and South-eastern Bank of Lake Erie, following the said Bank, until the
same shall be intersected by the Northern Boundary, granted by the Charter of the Province of Pensylvania, in case the same shall be so intersected;
and from thence along the said Northern and Western Boundaries of the
said Province, until the said Western Boundary strike the Ohio: But in case
the said Bank of the said Lake shall not be found to be so intersected then

following the said Bank until it shall arrive at that Point of the said Bank which shall be nearest to the North-western Angle of the said Province of Pensylvania, and thence, by a right Line, to the said North-western Angle of the said Province; and thence along the Western Boundary of the said Province, until it strike the River Ohio; and along the Bank of the said River, Westward, to the Banks of the Mississippi, and Northward to the Southern Boundary of the Territory granted to the Merchants Adventurers of England, trading to Hudson's Bay; and also all such Territories, Islands, and Countries which have, since the Tenth of February, One thousand seven hundred and sixty-three, been made Part of the Government of New-foundland, be, and they are hereby, during His Majesty's Pleasure, annexed to, and made Part and Parcel of, the Province of Quebec, as created and established by the said Royal Proclamation of the Seventh of October, One thousand seven hundred and sixty-three.

Provided always, That nothing herein contained, relative to the Boundary of the Province of Quebec, shall in anywise affect the Boundaries of any other Colony.

Provided always, and be it enacted, That nothing in this Act contained, shall extend, or be construed to extend, to make void, or to vary or alter any Right, Title, or Possession, derived under any Grant, Conveyance, or otherwise howsoever, of or to any Lands within the said Province, or the Provinces thereto adjoining; but that the same shall remain and be in Force, and have Effect, as if this Act had never been made.

And whereas the Provisions, made by the said Proclamation, in respect to the Civil Government of the said Province of Quebec and the Powers and Authorities given to the Governor and other Civil Officers of the said Province, by the Grants and Commissions issued in consequence thereof, have been found, upon Experience, to be inapplicable to the State and Circumstances of the said Province, the Inhabitants whereof amounted, at the Conquest, to above Sixty-five thousand Persons professing the Religion of the Church of Rome, and enjoying an established Form of Constitution and System of Laws, by which their Persons and Property had been protected, governed, and ordered, for a long Series of Years, from the First Establishment of the said Province of Canada; be it therefore further enacted by the Authority aforesaid, That the said Proclamation, so far as the same relates to the said Province of Quebec, and the Commission under the Authority whereof the Government of the said Province is at present administered, and all and every the Ordinance and Ordinances made by the Governor and Council of Quebec for the Time being, relative to the Civil Government and Administration of Justice in the said Province, and all Commissions to Judges and other Officers thereof, be, and the same are hereby revoked, annulled, and made void, from and after the First Day of May, One thousand seven hundred and seventy-five.

And, for the more perfect Security and Ease of the Minds of the Inhabitants of the said Province, it is hereby declared, That His Majesty's

Subjects, professing the Religion of the Church of <u>Rome</u> of and in the said Province of <u>Quebec</u>, may have, hold, and enjoy, the free Exercise of the Religion of the Church of <u>Rome</u>, subject to the King's Supremacy, declared and established by an Act, made in the First Year of the Reign of Queen <u>Elizabeth</u>, over all the Dominions and Countries which then did, or thereafter should belong, to the Imperial Crown of this Realm; and that the Clergy of the said Church may hold, receive, and enjoy, their accustomed Dues and Rights, with respect to such Persons only as shall profess the said Religion.

Provided nevertheless, That it shall be lawful for His Majesty, His Heirs or Successors, to make such Provision out of the rest of the said accustomed Dues and Rights, for the Encouragement of the Protestant Religion, and for the Maintenance and Support of a Protestant Clergy within the said Province, as he or they shall, from Time to Time, think necessary and expedient.

Provided always, and be it enacted, That no Person, professing the Religion of the Church of <u>Rome</u>, and residing in the said Province, shall be obliged to take the Oath required by the said Statute passed in the First Year of the Reign of Queen <u>Elizabeth</u>, or any other Oaths substituted by any other Act in the Place thereof; but that every such Person who, by the said Statute is required to take the Oath therein mentioned, shall be obliged, and is hereby required, to take and subscribe the following Oath before the Governor, or such other Person in such Court of Record as His Majesty shall appoint, who are hereby authorised to administer the same; <u>videticet</u>,

I A.B. do sincerely promise and swear, That I will be faithful, and bear true Allegiance to His Majesty King George, and him will defend to the utmost of my Power, against all traiterous Conspiracies, and Attempts whatsoever, which shall be made against His Person, Crown and Dignity; and I will do my utmost Endeavour to disclose and make known to His Majesty, His Heirs and Successors, all Treasons, and traiterous Conspiracies, and Attempts, which I shall know to be against Him, or any of Them; and all this I do swear without any Equivocation, mental Evasion, or secret Reservation, and renouncing all Pardons and Dispensations from any Power or Person whomsoever to the Contrary.

So Help Me GOD.

And every such Person, who shall neglect or refuse to take the said Oath before mentioned, shall incur and be liable to the same Penalties, Forfeitures, Disabilities, and Incapacities, as he would have incurred and been liable to for neglecting or refusing to take the Oath required by the said Statute passed in the First Year of the Reign of Queen <u>Elizabeth</u>.

And be it further enacted by the Authority aforesaid, That all His Majesty's Canadian Subjects, within the Province of Quebec, the religious Orders and Communities only expected, may also hold and enjoy their Property and Possessions, together with all Customs and Usages relative thereto, and all other their Civil Rights, in as large, ample, and beneficial

Manner, as if the said Proclamation, Commissions, Ordinances, and other Acts and Instruments, had not been made, and as may consist with their Allegiance to His Majesty, and Subjection to the Crown and Parliament of Great Britain; and that in all Matters of Controversy, relative to Property and Civil Rights, Resort shall be had to the Laws of Canada, as the Rule for the Decision of the same; and all Causes that shall hereafter be instituted in any of the Courts of Justice, to be appointed within and for the said Province, by His Majesty, His Heirs and Successors, shall, with respect to such Property and Rights, be determined agreeably to the said Laws and Customs of Canada, until they shall be varied or altered by any Ordinances, that shall, from Time to Time, be passed in the said Province by the Governor, Lieutenant Governor, or Commander in Chief, for the Time being, by and with the Advice and Consent of the Legislative Council of the same, to be appointed in Manner herein-after mentioned.

Provided also, That it shall and may be lawful to and for every Person that is Owner of any Lands, Goods, or Credits, in the said Province, and that has a Right to alienate the said Lands, Goods, or Credits, in his or her Life-time, by Deed of Sale, Gift, or otherwise, to devise or bequeath the same at his or her Death, by his or her last Will and Testament, any Law Usage, or Custom, heretofore or now prevailing in the Province, to the Contrary hereof in any-wise notwithstanding; such Will be executed, either according to the Laws of Canada, or according to the Forms prescribed by the Laws of England.

And whereas the Certainty and Lenity of the Criminal Law of England, and the Benefits and Advantages resulting from the Use of it, have been sensibly felt by the Inhabitants, from an Experience of more than Nine Years, during which it has been uniformly administered; be it therefore further enacted by the Authority aforesaid, That the same shall continue to be administered, and shall be observed as Law in the Province of Quebec, as well in the Description and Quality of the Offense as in the Method of Prosecution and Trial; and the Punishments and Forfeitures thereby inflicted to the exclusion of every other Rule of Criminal Law, or Mode of Proceeding thereon, which did or might prevail in the said Province before the Year of Our Lord One thousand seven hundred and sixty-four; any Thing in this Act to the Contrary thereof in any Respect notwithstanding; subject nevertheless to such Alterations and Amendments as the Governor, Lieutenant-governor, or Commander in Chief for the Time being, by and with the Advice and Consent of the legislative Council of the said Province, hereafter to be appointed, shall, from Time to Time, cause to be made therein, in Manner herein-after directed.

And whereas it may be necessary to ordain many Regulations for the future Welfare and good Government of the Province of Quebec, the Occasions of which cannot now be foreseen, nor, without much Delay and Inconvenience, be provided for without intrusting that Authority, for a certain Time, and under proper Restrictions, to Persons resident there: And whereas it is at present inexpedient to call an Assembly; be it therefore enacted by the Authority aforesaid, That it shall and may be lawful for His Majesty, His Heirs and Successors, by Warrant under His or Their Signet or Sign Manual, and with the Advice of the Privy Council, to constitute and appoint a Council for the Affairs of the Province of Quebec, to consist of such Persons resident there, not exceeding Twenty-three, nor less than Seventeen, as His Majesty, His Heirs and Successors, shall be pleased to appoint; and, upon the Death, Removal, or Absence of any of the Members of the said Council, in like Manner to constitute and appoint such and so many other Person or Persons as shall be necessary to supply the Vacancy or Vacancies; which Council, so appointed and nominated, or the major Part thereof, shall have Power and Authority to make Ordinances for the Peace, Welfare, and good Government, of the said Province, with the Consent of His Majesty's Governor, or, in his Absence, of the Lieutenant-governor, or Commander in Chief for the Time being.

Provided always, That nothing in this Act contained shall extend to authorise or impower the said legislative Council to lay any Taxes or Duties within the said Province, such Rates and Taxes only excepted as the Inhabitants of any Town or District within the said Province may be authorised by the said Council to assess, levy, and apply, within the said Town or District, for the Purpose of making Roads, erecting and repairing publick Buildings, or for any other Purpose respecting the local Convenience and Oeconomy of such Town or District.

Provided also, and be it enacted by the Authority aforesaid, That every Ordinance so to be made, shall, within Six Months, be transmitted by the Governor, or, in his Absence, by the Lieutenant-governor, or Commander in Chief for the Time being, and laid before His Majesty for His Royal Approbation; and if His Majesty shall think fit to disallow thereof, the same shall cease and be void from the Time that His Majesty's Order in Council thereupon shall be promulgated at Quebec.

Provided also, That no Ordinance shall bw passed at any Meeting of the Council where less than a Majority of the whole Council is present, or at any Time except between the First Day of January and First Day of May, unless upon some urgent Occasion, in which Case every Member thereof resident at Quebec, or within Fifty Miles thereof, shall be personally summoned by the Governor, or, in his Absence, by the Lieutenant-governor, or Commander in Chief for the Time being, to attend the same.

And be it further enacted by the Authority aforesaid, That nothing herein contained shall extend, or be construed to extend, to prevent or hinder His Majesty, His Heirs and Successors, by His or Their Letters Patent under the Great Seal of Great Britain, from erecting, constituting, and appointing, such Courts of Criminal, Civil, and Ecclesiastical Jurisdiction within and for the said Province of Quebec, and appointing, from Time to Time, the Judges and Officers thereof, as His Majesty, His Heirs and Successors, shall think necessary and proper for the Circumstances of the said province.

Provided always, and it is hereby enacted, That nothing in this Act contained shall extend, or be construed to extend, to repeal or make void, within the said Province of <u>Quebec</u>, any Act or Acts of the Parliament of <u>Great Britain</u> heretofore made, for prohibiting, restraining, or regulating, the Trade or Commerce of His Majesty's Colonies and Plantations in <u>America</u>; but that all and every the said Acts, and also all Acts of Parliament heretofore made concerning or respecting the said Colonies and Plantations, shall be, and are hereby declared to be, in Force, within the said Province of <u>Quebec,</u> and every Part thereof.

Finis.

THE CONSTITUTIONAL ACT OF 1791.

Anno Tricesimo Primo

GEORGEII III. REGIS.

CAP. XXXI.

An Act to repeal certain Parts of an Act, passed in the Fourteenth Year of His Majesty's Reign, intituled, An Act for making more effectual Provision for the Government of the Province
of Quebec, in North America; and to make further Provision for
the Government of the said Province.

Whereas an Act was passed in the Fourteenth Year of the Reign of
His present Majesty, intituled, An Act for making more effectual Provision for the Government of the Province of Quebec in North America: And
whereas the said Act is in many Respects inapplicable to the present Condition and Circumstances of the said Province: And whereas it is expedient and necessary that further Provision should now be made for the good
Government and Prosperity thereof: May it therefore please Your most
Excellent Majesty that it may be enacted; and be it enacted by the King's
most Excellent Majesty, by and with the Advice and Consent of the Lords
Spiritual and Temporal, and Commons, in this present Parliament assembled, and by the Authority of the same, That so much of the said Act as
in any Manner relates to the Appointment of a Council for the Affairs of
the said Province of Quebec, or to the Power given by the said Act to the
said Council, or to the major Part of them, to make Ordinances for the
Peace, Welfare, and good Government of the said Province, with the Consent of His Majesty's Governor, Lieutenant Governor, or Commander in
Chief for the Time being, shall be, and the same is hereby repealed.
    II. And whereas His Majesty has been pleased to signify, by His Mes-
sage to both Houses of Parliament, His Royal Intention to divide His Province of Quebec into Two separate Provinces, to be called The Province
of Upper Canada and The Province of Lower Canada; be it enacted by the
Authority aforesaid, That there shall be within each of the said Provinces
respectively a Legislative Council, and an Assembly, to be severally com
posed and constituted in the Manner herein-after described; and that in
each of the said Provinces respectively His Majesty, His Heirs or Successors, shall have Power, during the Continuance of this Act, by and
with the Advice and Consent of the Legislative Council and Assembly of
such Provinces respectively, to make Laws for the Peace, Welfare, and
good Government thereof, such Laws not being repugnant to this Act; and
that all such Laws, being passed by the Legislative Council and Assembly
of either of the said Provinces respectively, and assented to by His Ma-

jesty, His Heirs or Successors, or assented to in His Majesty's Name, by such Person as His Majesty, His Heirs or Successors, shall from Time to Time appoint to be the Governor, or Lieutenant Governor, of such Province, or by such Person as His Majest, His Heirs or Successors, shall from Time to Time appoint to administer the Government within the same, shall be, and the same are hereby declared to be, by virtue of and under the Authority of this Act, valid and binding to all Intents and Purposes whatever, within the Province in which the same shall have been so passed.

III. And be it further enacted by the Authority aforesaid, That for the Purpose of constituting such Legislative Council as aforesaid in each of the said Provinces respectively, it shall and may be lawful for His Majesty, His Heirs or Successors, by an Instrument under His or their Sign Manual, to authorize and direct the Governor or Lieutenant Governor, or Person administering the Government in each of the said Provinces respectively, within the Time herein-after mentioned, in His Majesty's Name, and by an Instrument under the Great Seal of such Province, to summon to the said Legislative Council, to be established in each of the said Provinces respectively, a sufficient Number of discreet and proper Persons, being not fewer than Seven to the Legislative Council for the Province of Upper Canada, and not fewer than Fifteen to the Legislative Council for the Province of Lower Canada; and that it shall also be lawful for His Majesty, His Heirs or Successors, from Time to Time, by an Instrument under His or their Sign Manual, to authorize and direct the Governor or Lieutenant Governor, or Person administering the Government in each of the said Provinces respectively, to summon to the Legislative Council of such Province, in like Manner, such other Person or Persons as His Majesty, His Heirs or Successors, shall think fit; and that every Person who shall be so summoned to the Legislative Council of either of the said Provinces respectively, shall thereby become a Member of such Legislative Council to which he shall have been so summoned.

IV. Provided always, and be it enacted by the Authority aforesaid, That no Person shall be summoned to the said Legislative Council, in either of the said Provinces, who shall not be of the full Age of Twenty-one Years, and a natural-born Subject of His Majesty, or a Subject of His Majesty naturalized by Act of the British Parliament, or a Subject of His Majesty, having become such by the Conquest and Cession of the Province of Canada.

V. And be it further enacted by the Authority aforesaid, That every Member of each of the said Legislative Councils shall hold his Seat therein after contained for vacating the same, in the Cases herein-after specified.

VI. And be it further enacted by the Authority aforesaid, That whenever His Majesty, His Heirs or Successors, shall think proper to confer upon any Subject of the Crown of Great Britain, by Letters Patent under

the Great Seal of either of the said Provinces, any Hereditary Title of
Honour, Rank, or Dignity of such Province, descendible according to any
Course of Descent limited in such Letters Patent, it shall and may be lawful for His Majesty, His Heirs or Successors, to annex thereto, by the
said Letters Patent, if His Majesty, His Heirs or Successors, shall so
think fit, an Hereditary Right of being summoned to the Legislative Council of such Province, descendible according to the Course of Descent so
limited with respect to such Title, Rank, or Dignity; and that every Person on whom such Right shall be so conferred, or to whom such Right
shall severally so descend, shall thereupon be entitled to demand from
the Governor, Lieutenant Governor, or Person administering the Government of such Province, his Writ of Summons to such Legislative Council,
at any Time after he shall have attained the Age of Twenty-one Years,
subject nevertheless to the Provisions herein-after contained.

VII.   Provided always, and be it further enacted by the Authority
aforesaid, That when and so often as any Person to whom such Hereditary
Right shall have descended shall, without the Permission of His Majesty,
His Heir or Successors, signified to the Legislative Council of the Province by the Governor, Lieutenant Governor, or Person administering the
Government there, have been absent from the said Province for the Space
of Four Years continually, at any Time between the Date of his succeeding to such Right and the Time of his applying for such Writ of Summons,
if he shall have been of the Age of Twenty-one Years or upwards at the
Time of his so succeeding, or at any Time between the Date of his at-
taining the said Age and the Time of his so applying, if he shall not have
been of the said Age at the Time of his so succeeding; and also when and
so often as any such Person shall at any Time, before his applying for
such Writ of Summons, have taken any Oath of Allegiance or Obedience
to any Foreign Prince or Power, in every such Case such Person shall not
be entitled to receive any Writ of Summons to the Legislative Council by
virtue of such Hereditary Right, unless His Majesty, His Heirs or Successors, shall at any Time think fit, by Instrument under His or their
Sign Manual, to direct that such Person shall be summoned to the said
Council; and the Governor, Lieutenant Governor, or Person administering the Government in the said Provinces respectively, is hereby authorized and required, previous to granting such Writ of Summons to any
Person so applying for the same, to interrogate such Person upon Oath
touching the said several Particulars, before such executive Council as
shall have been appointed by His Majesty, His Heirs or Successors, within such Province, for the Affairs thereof.

VIII.   Provided also, and be it further enacted by the Authority aforesaid That   if any Member of the Legislative Councils of either of the said
Provinces respectively shall leave such Province and shall reside out of
the same for the Space of Four Years continually, without the Permission
of His Majesty, His Heirs or Successors, signified to such Legislative

Council by the Governor or Lieutentant Governor, or Person administering
His Majesty's Government there, or for the Space of Two Years continually, without the like Permission, or the Permission of the Governor,
Lieutenant Governor, or Person administering the Government of such
Province, signified to such Legislative Council in the Manner aforesaid;
or if any such Member shall take any Oath of Allegiance or Obedience to
any Foreign Prince or Power; his Seat in such Council shall thereby become
vacant.

IX. Provided also, and be it further enacted by the Authority afore-
said, That in every Case where a Writ of Summons to such Legislative
Council shall have been lawfully withheld from any Person to whom such
Hereditary Right as aforesaid shall have descended, by Reason of such Absence from the Province as aforesaid, or of his having taken an Oath of
Allegiance or Obedience to any Foreign Prince or Power, and also in every
Case where the Seat in such Council of any Member thereof, having such
Hereditary Right as aforesaid, shall have been vacated by Reason of any of
the Causes herein-before specified, such Hereditary Right shall remain
suspended during the Life of such Person, unless His Majesty, His Heirs
or Successors, shall afterwards think fit to direct that he be summoned
to such Council; but that on the Death of such Person such Right, subject
to the Provisions herein contained, shall descend to the Person who shall
next be entitled thereto, according to the Course of Descent limited in the
Letters Patent by which the same shall have been originally conferred.

X. Provided also, and be it further enacted by the Authority aforesaid, That if any Member of either of the said Legislative Councils shall
be attainted for Treason in any Court of Law within any of His Majesty's
Dominions, his Seat in such Council shall thereby become vacant, and any
such Hereditary Right as aforesaid then vested in such Person, or to be
derived to any other Persons through him, shall be utterly forfeited and
extinguished.

XI. Provided also, and be it further enacted by the Authority aforesaid, That whenever any Question shall arise respecting the Right of any
Person to be summoned to either of the said Legislative Councils respectively, or respecting the Vacancy of the Seat in such Legislative Council
of any Person having been summoned thereto, every such Question shall,
by the Governor or Lieutenant Governor of the Province, or by the Person
administering the Government there, be referred to such Legislative Council, to be by the said Coujcil heard and determined; and that it shall and
may be lawful either for the Person desiring such Writ of Summons, or
respecting whose Seat such Question shall have arisen, or for His Majesty's Attorney General of such Province in His Majesty's Name, to appeal
from the Determination of the said Council, in such Case, to His Majesty
in His Parliament of Great Britain; and that the Judgement thereon of His
Majesty in His said Parliament shall be final and conclusive to all Intents
and Purposes whatever.

XII. And be it further enacted by the Authority aforesaid, That the Governor or Lieutenant Governor of the said Provinces respectively, or the Person administering His Majesty's Government therein respectively, shall have Power and Authority from Time to Time, by an Instrument under the Great Seal of such Province, to constitute, appoint, and remove the Speakers of the Legislative Councils of such Provinces respectively.

XIII. And be it further enacted by the Authority aforesaid, That, for the Purpose of constituting such Assembly as aforesaid, in each of the said Provinces respectively, it shall and may be lawful for His Majesty, His Heirs or Successors, by an Instrument under His or their Sign Manual, to authorize and direct the Governor or Lieutenant Governor, or Person administering the Government in each of the said Provinces respectively, within the Time herein-after mentioned, and thereafter from Time to Time, as Occasion shall require, in His Majesty's Name, and by an Instrument Assembly in and for such Province.

XIV. And be it further enacted by the Authority aforesaid, That, for the Purpose of electing the Members of such Assemblies respectively, it shall and may be lawful for His Majesty, His Heirs or Successors, by an Instrument under His or their Sign Manual, to authorize the Governor or Lieutenant Governor of each of the said Provinces respectively, or the Person administering the Government therein, within the Time hereinafter mentioned, to issue a Proclamation dividing such Province into Districts, or Counties, or Circles, and Towns or Townships, and appointing the Limits thereof, and declaring and appointing the Number of Representatives to be chosen by each of such Districts, or Counties, or Circles, and Towns or Townships respectively; and that it shall also be lawful for His Majesty, His Heirs or Successors, to authorize such Governor or Lieutenant Governor, or Person administering the Government from Time to Time to nominate and appoint proper Persons to execute the Office of returning Officer in each of the said Districts, or Counties, or Circles, and Towns or Townships respectively; and that such Division of the said Province into Districts, or Counties, or Circles, and Towns or Townships, and such Declaration and Appointment of the Number of Representatives to be chosen by each of the said Districts, or Counties, or Circles, and To Towns or Townships respectively, and also such Nomination and Appointment of Returning Officers in the same, shall be valid and effectual to all the Purposes of this Act, unless it shall at any Time be otherwise provided by any Act of the Legislative Council and Assembly of the Province assented to by His Majesty, His Heirs or Successors.

XV. Provided nevertheless, and be it further enacted by the Authority aforesaid, That the Provision herein-before contained, for impowering the Governor, Lieutenant Governor, or Person administering the Government of the said Provinces respectively, under such Authority as aforesaid from His Majesty, His Heirs or Successors, from Time to Time, to nominate and appoint proper Persons to execute the Office of Returning Officer in the said Districts, Counties, Circles, and Towns or Townships, shall remain and continue in Force in each of the said Provinces respectively, for the Term of Two Years, from and after the Commencement of this Act within such Province, and no longer; but subject nevertheless to be sooner repealed or varied by any Act of the Legislative Council and Assembly of the Province, assented to by His Majesty, His Heirs or Successors.

XVI. Provided always, and be it further enacted by the Authority aforesaid, That no Person shall be obliged to execute the said Office of Returning Officer for any longer Time than One Year, or oftener than Once, unless it whall at any Time be otherwise provided by any Act of the Legislative Council and Assembly of the Province, assented to by His Majesty, His Heirs or Successors.

XVII. Provided also, and be it enacted by the Authority aforesaid, That the whole Number of Members to be chosen in the Province of Upper Canada shall not be less than Sixteen, and that the whole Number of Members to be chosen in the Province of Lower Canada shall not be less than Fifty.

XVIII. And be it further enacted by the Authority aforesaid, That Writs for the Election of Members to serve in the said Assemblies respectively shall be issued by the Governor, Lieutenant Governor, or Person administering His Majesty's Government within the said Provinces respectively, within Fourteen Days after the sealing of such Instrument as aforesaid for summoning and calling together such Assembly, and that such Writs shall be directed to the respective Returning Officers of the said Districts, or Counties, or Circles, and Towns or Townships, and that such Writs shall be made returnable within Fifty Days at farthest from the Day on which they shall bear Date, unless it shall at any Time be otherwise provided by any Act of the Legislative Council and Assembly of the Province, assented to by His Majesty, His Heirs or Successors; and that Writs shall in like Manner and Form be issued for the Election of Members in the Case of any Vacancy which shall happen by the Death of the Person chosen, or by his being summoned to the Legislative Council of either Province, and that such Writs shall be made returnable within Fifty Days at farthest from the Day on which they shall bear Date, unless it shall at any Time be otherwise provided by any Act of the Legislative Council and Assembly of the Province, assented to by His Majesty, His Heirs or Successors; and that in the Case of any such Vacancy which shall happen by the Death of the Person chosen, or by Reason of his being so summoned as aforesaid, the Writ for the Election of a new Member shall be issued within Six Days after the same shall be made known to the proper Office for issuing such Writs of Election.

XIX. And be it further enacted by the Authority aforesaid, That all and every the Returning Officers so appointed as aforesaid, to whom any such Writs as aforesaid shall be directed, shall, and they are hereby authorized and required duly to execute such Writs.

XX. And be it further enacted by the Authority aforesaid, That the Members for the several Districts, or Counties, or Circles of the said Provinces respectively, shall be chosen by the Majority of Votes of such Persons as shall severally be possessed, for their own Use and Benefit, of Lands or Tenements within such District, or County, or Circle, as the Case shall be, such Lands being by them held in Freehold, or in Fief, or in Roture, or by Certificate derived under the Authority of the Governor and Council of the Province of Quebec, and being of the yearly Value of Forty Shillings Sterling, or upwards, over and above all Rents and Charges payable out of or in respect of the same; and that the Members for the several Towns or Townships within the said Provinces respectively shall be chosen by the Majority of Votes of such Persons as either shall severally be possessed, for their own Use and Benefit, of a Dwelling House and Lot of Ground in such Town or Township, such Dwelling House and Lot of Ground being by them held in like Manner as aforesaid, and being of the yearly Value of Five Pounds Sterling, or upwards, or, as having been resident within the said Town or Township for the Space of Twelve Calendar Months next before the Date of the Writ of Summons for the Election, shall bona fide have paid One Year's Rent for the Dwelling House in which they shall have so resided, at the Rate of Ten Pounds Sterling per Annum, or upwards.

XXI. Provided always, and be it further enacted by the Authority aforesaid, That no Person shall be capable of being elected a Member to serve in either of the said Assemblies, or of sitting or voting therein, who shall be a Member of either of the said Legislative Councils to be established as aforesaid in the said Two Provinces, or who shall be a Minister of the Church of England, or a Minister, Priest, Ecclesiastic, or Teacher, either according to the Rites of the Church of Rome, or under any other Form or Profession of Religious Faith or Worship.

XXII. Provided also, and be it further enacted by the Authority aforesaid, That no Person shall be capable of voting at any Election of a Member to serve in such Assembly, in either of the said Provinces, or of being elected at any such Election, who shall not be of the full Age of Twenty-one Years, and a natural-born Subject of His Majesty, or a Subject of His Majesty naturalized by Act of the British Parliament, or a Subject of His Majesty, having become such by the Conquest and Cession of the Province of Canada.

XXIII. And be it also enacted by the Authority aforesaid, That no Person shall be capable of voting at any Election of a Member to serve in such Assembly, in either of the said Provinces, or of being elected at any such Election, who shall have been attainted for Treason or Felony in any Court of Law within any of His Majesty's Dominions, or who shall be within any Description of Persons disqualified by any Act of the Legislative Council and Assembly of the Province, assented to by His Majesty, His Heirs or Successors.

XXIV.   Provided also, and be it further enacted by the Authority aforesaid, That every Voter, before he is admitted to give his Vote at any such Election, shall, if required by any of the Candidates or by the Returning Officer, take the following Oath, which shall be administered in the English or French Language, as the Case may require:

I. A.B. do declare and testify, in the Presence of Almighty God, That I am, to the best of my Knowledge and Belief, of the full Age of Twenty-one Years, and that I have not voted before at this Election.

And that every such Person shall also, if so required as aforesaid, make Oath, previous to his being admitted to vote, that he is, to the best of his Knowledge and Belief, duly possessed of such Lands and Tenements, or of such a Dwelling House and Lot of Ground, or that he has bona fide been so resident, and paid such Rent for his Dwelling House, as entitles him, according to the Provisions of this Act, to give his Vote at such Election for the County, or District, or Circle, or for the Town or Township for which he shall offer the same.

XXV.   And be it further enacted by the Authority aforesaid, That it shall and may be lawful for His Majesty, His Heirs or Successors, to authorize the Governor or Lieutenant Governor, or Person administering the Government within each of the said Provinces respectively, to fix the Time and Place of holding such Elections, giving not less than Eight Days Notice of such Time, subject nevertheless to such Provisions as may hereafter be made in these Respects by any Act of the Legislative Council and Assembly of the Province, assented to by His Majesty, His Heirs or Successors.

XXVI.   And be it further enacted by the Authority aforesaid, That it shall and may be lawful for His Majesty, His Heirs or Successors, to authorize the Governor or Lieutenant Governor of each of the said Provinces respectively, or the Person administering the Government therein, to fix the Places and Times of holding the First and every other Session of the Legislative Council and Assembly of such Province, giving due and sufficient Notice thereof, and to prorogue the same from Time to Time, and to dissolve the same, by Proclamation or otherwise, whenever he shall judge it necessary or expedient.

XXVII.   Provided always, and be it enacted by the Authority aforesaid, That the said Legislative Council and Assembly, in each of the said Provinces, shall be called together Once at the least in every Twelve Calendar Months, and that every Assembly shall continue for Four Years from the Day of the Return of the Writs for chusing the same, and no longer, subject nevertheless to be sooner prorogued or dissolved by the Governor or Lieutenant Governor of the Province, or Person administering His Majesty's Government therein.

XXVIII.   And be it further enacted by the Authority aforesaid, That all Questions which shall arise in the said Legislative Councils or Assemblies respectively shall be decided by the Majority of Voices of such Members as shall be present; and that in all Cases wherethe Voices shall be

equal, the Speaker of such Council or Assembly, as the Case shall be,
shall have a casting Voice.

XXIX. Provided always, and be it enacted by the Authority aforesaid,
that no Member, either of the Legislative Council or Assembly, in either
of the said Provinces, shall be permitted to sit or to vote therein until he
shall have taken and subscribed the following Oath, either before the Governor or Lieutenant Governor of such Province, or Person administering
the Government therein, or before some Person or Persons authorized by
the said Govenor or Lietuenant Governor, or other Person as aforesaid,
to administer such Oath, and that the same shall be administered in the
English or French Language, as the Case shall require:
I A.B., do sincerely promise and swear, That I will be faithful, and bear
true Allegiance to His Majesty King George, as lawful Sovereign of the
Kingdom of Great Britain, and of these Provinces dependant on and belonging to the said Kingdom; and that I will defend Him to the utmost of my
Power against all traiterous Conspiracies and Attempts whatever which
shall be made against His Person, Crown, and Dignity; and that I will do
my utmost Endeavour to disclose and make known to His Majesty, His
Heirs or Successors, all Treasons and traiterous Conspiracies and Attempts which I shall know to be against Him, or any of them: and all this
I do swear without any Equivocation, mental Evasion, or secret Reservation, and renouncing all Pardons and Dispensations from any Person or
Power whatever to the contrary.

So help me GOD.

XXX. And be it further enacted by the Authority aforesaid, That
whenever any Bill which has been passed by the Legislative Council, and
by the House of Assembly, in either of the said Provinces respectively,
shall be presented, for His Majesty's Assent, to the Governor or Lieutenant Governor of such Province, or to the Person administering His Majesty's Government therein, such Governor or Lieutenant Governor, or
Person administering the Government, shall, and he is hereby authorized
and required to declare, according to his Discretion, but subject nevertheless to the Provisions contained in this Act, and to such Instructions as
may from Time to Time be given in that Behalf by His Majesty, His Heirs
or Successors, that he assents to such Bill in His Majesty's Name, or that
he withholds His Majesty's Assent from such Bill, or that he reserves such
Bill for the Signification of His Majesty's Pleasure thereon.

XXXI. Provided always, and be it further enacted by the Authority
aforesaid, That whenever any Bill, which shall have been so presented for
His Majesty's Assent to such Governor, Lieutenant Governor, or Person
administering the Government, shall, by such Governor, Lieutenant Governor, or Person administering the Government, have been assented to in
His Majesty's Name, such Governor, Lieutenant Governor, or Person as
aforesaid, shall, and he is hereb required, by the first convenient Opportunity, to transmit to One of His Majesty's principal Secretaries of State
an authentick Copy of such Bill so assented to; and that it shall and may be

lawful, at any Time within Two Years after such Bill shall have been so received by such Secretary of State, for His Majesty, His Heirs or Successors, by His or their Order in Council, to declare His or their Disallowance of such Bill, and that such Disallowance, together with a Certificate, under the Hand and Seal of such Secretary of State, testifying the Day on which such Bill was received as aforesaid, being signified by such Governor, Lieutenant Governor, or Person administering the Government, to the Legislative Council and Assembly of such Province, or by Proclamation, shall make void and annul the same, from and after the Date of such Signification.

XXXII. And be it further enacted by the Authority aforesaid, That no such Bill, which shall be so reserved for the Signification of His Majesty's Pleasure thereon, shall have any Force or Authority within either of the said Provinces respectively, until the Governor or Lieutenant Governor, or Person administering the Government, shall signify, either by Speech or Message, to the Legislative Council and Assembly of such Province, or by Proclamation, that such Bill has been laid before His Majesty in Council, and that His Majesty has been pleased to assent to the same; and that an Entry shall be made, in the Journals of the said Legislative Council, of every such Speech, Message, or Proclamation; and a Duplicate thereof, duly attested, shall be delivered to the proper Officer, to be kept amongst the publick Records of the Province: And that no such Bill, which shall be so reserved as aforesaid, shall have any Force or Authority within either of the said Provinces respectively, unless His Majesty's As Assent thereto shall have been so signified as aforesaid, within the Space of Two Years from the Day on which such Bill shall have been presented for His Majesty's Assent to the Governor, Lieutenant Governor, or Person administering the Government of such Province.

XXXII. And be it further enacted by the Authority aforesaid, That all Laws, Statutes, and Ordinances, which shall be in Force on the Day to be fixed in the Manner herein-after directed for the Commencement of this Act, within the said Provinces, or either of them, or in any Part thereof respectively, shall remain and continue to be of the same Force, Authority, and Effect, in each of the said Provinces respectively, as if this Act had not been made, and as if the said Province of Quebec had not been divided; except in so far as the same are expressly repealed or varied by this Act, or in so far as the same shall or may hereafter, by virtue of and under the Authority of this Act, be repealed or varied by His Majesty, His Heirs or Successors, by and with the Advice and Consent of the Legislative Councils and Assemblies of the said Provinces respectively, or in so far as the same may be repealed or varied by such temporary Laws or Ordinances as may be made in the Manner herein-after specified.

XXXIV. And whereas by an Ordinance passed in the Province of Quebec, the Governor and Council of the said Province were constituted a Court of Civil Jurisdiction, for hearing and determining Appeals in certain Cases therein specified, be it further enacted by the Authority aforesaid, That the Governor, or Lieutenant Governor, or Person administering the Government of each of the said Provinces respectively, together with such executive Council as shall be appointed by His Majesty for the Affairs of such Province shall be a Court of Civil Jurisdiction within each of the said Provinces respectively, for hearing and determining Appeals within the same, in the like Cases, and in the like Manner and Form, and subject to such Appeal therefrom, as such Appeals might before the passing of this Act have been heard and determined by the Governor and Council of the Province of Quebec; but subject nevertheless to such further or other Provisions as may be made in this Behalf, by any Act of the Legislative Council and Assembly of either of the said Provinces respectively, assented to by His Majesty, His Heirs or Successors.

XXXV. And whereas, by the above-mentioned Act, passed in the Fourteenth Year of the Reign of His present Majesty, it was declared, That the Clergy of the Church of Rome, in the Province of Quebec, might hold, receive, and enjoy their accustomed Dues and Rights, with respect to such Persons only as should profess the said Religion; provided nevertheless, that it should be lawful for His Majesty, His Heirs or Successors, to make such Provision out of the rest of the said accustomed Dues and Rights, for the Encouragement of the Protestant Religion, and for the Maintenance and Support of a Protestant Clergy within the said Province, as he or they should from Time to Time think necessary and expedient: And whereas by His Majesty's Royal Instructions, given under His Majesty's Royal Sign Manual on the Third Day of January, in the Year of our Lord One thousand seven hundred and seventy-five, to Guy Carleton Esquire, now Lord Dorchester, at that Time His Majesty's Captain General and Governor in Chief in and over His Majesty's Province of Quebec, His Majesty was pleased, amongst other Tings, to direct, "That no Incumbent professing the "Religion of the Church of Rome, appointed to any Parish in the said "Province, should be entitled to receive any Tythes for Lands or Possessions "occupied by a Protestant, but that such Tythes should be received by "such Persons as the said Guy Carleton Esquire, His Majesty's Captain "General and Governor in Chief in and over His Majesty's said Province of Quebec, should appoint, and should be reserved in the Hands of his Majesty's Receiver General of the said Province, for the Support of a Protestant Clergy in His Majesty's said Province, to be actually resident within the same, and not otherwise, according to such Directions as the said Guy Carleton Esquire, His Majesty's Captain General and Governor in Chief in and over His Majesty's said Province, should receive from His Majesty in that Behalf; and that in like Manner all growing Rents and Profits of a vacant Benefice should, during such Vacancy, be reserved for and applied to the like Uses:" And whereas His Majesty's Pleasure has likewise been signified to the same Effect in His Majesty's Royal Instructions, given in like Manner to Sire Frederick Haldimand Knight of the Most Honourable Order of the Bath, late His Majesty's Captain General and Governor in Chief in and over His Majesty's said Province of Quebec, and also in His Majesty's Royal Instructions, given in like Manner to the said Right Honourable Guy Lord Dorchester, now His Majesty's Captain General and Governor in Chief in and over His Majesty's said Province of Quebec; be it enacted by the Authority aforesaid, That the said Declaration and Provision contained in the said above-mentioned Act, and also the said Provision so made by His Majesty in consequence thereof, by His Instructions above recited, shall remain and continue to be of full Force and Effect in each of the said Two Provinces of Upper Canada and Lower Canada respectively, except in so far as the said Declaration or Provisions respectively, or any Part thereof, shall be expressly varied or repealed by any Act or Acts which may be passed by the Legislative Council and Assembly of the said Provinces respectively, and assented to by His Majesty, His Heirs or Successors, under the Restriction herein-after provided.

XXXVI. And whereas His Majesty has been graciously pleased, by Message to both Houses of Parliament, to express His Royal Desire to be enabled to make a permanent Appropriation of Lands in the said Provinces, for the Support and Maintenance of a Protestant Clergy within the same, in Proportion to such Lands as have been already granted within the same by His Majesty: And whereas His Majesty has been graciously pleased, by His said Message, further to signify His Royal Desire that such Provision may be made, with respect to all future Grants of Land within the said Provinces respectively, as may best conduce to the due and sufficient Support and Maintenance of a Protestant Clergy within the said Provinces, in Proporltion to such Increase as may happen in the Population and Cultivation thereof: Therefore, for the Purpose of more effectually fulfilling His Majesty's gracious Intentions as aforesaid, and of providing for the due Execution of the same in all Time to come, be it enacted by the Authority aforesaid, That it shall and may be lawful for His Majesty, His Heirs or Successors, to authorize the Governor or Lieutenant Governor of each of the said Provinces respectively, or the Person administering the Government therein, to make, from and out of the Lands of the Crown within such Provinces, such Allotment and Appropriation of Lands, for the Support and Maintenance of a Protestant Clergy within the same, as may bear a due Proportion to the Amount of such Lands within the same as have at any Time been granted by or under the Authority of His Majesty: And that whenever any Grant of Lands within either of the said Provinces shall hereafter be made, by or under the Authority of His Majesty, His Heirs or Successors, there shall at the same Time be made, in respect of the same, a proportionable Allotment and Appropriation of Lands for the above-mentioned Purpose, within the Township or Parish to which such Lands so to be granted shall appertain or be annexed, or as nearly adjacent thereto as Circumstances will admit; and that no such Grant shall be valid or effectual unless the same shall contain a Specification of the Lands so allotted and appropriated, in respect of the Lands to be thereby granted; and that such Lands, so allotted and appropriated, shall be, as nearly as the Circumstances and Nature of the Case will admit, of the like Quality as the Lands in respect of which the same are so allotted and appropriated, and shall be, as nearly as the same can be estimated at the Time of making such Grant, equal in Value to the Seventh Part of the Lands so granted.

XXXVII. And be it further enacted by the Authority aforesaid, That all and every the Rents, Profits or Emoluments, which may at any Time arise from such Lands so allotted and appropriated as aforesaid, shall be applicable solely to the Maintenance and Support of a Protestant Clergy within the Province in which the same shall be situated, and to no other Use or Purpose whatever.

XXXVIII. And be it further enacted by the Authority aforesaid, That it shall and may be lawful for His Majesty, His Heirs or Successors, to authorize the Governor or Lieutenant Governor of each of the said Provinces respectively, or the Person administering the Government therein, from Time to Time, with the Advice of such Executive Council as shall have been appointed by His Majesty, His Heirs or Successors, within such Province, for the Affairs thereof, to constitute and erect, within every Township or Parish which now is or hereafter may be formed, constituted, or erected within such Province, One or more Parsonage or Rectory, or Parsonages or Rectories, according to the Establishment of the Church of England; and from Time to Time, by an Instrument under the Great Seal of such Province, to endow every such Parsonage or Rectory with so much or such Part of the Lands so allotted and appropriated as aforesaid, in respect of any Lands within such Township or Parish, which shall have been granted subsequent to the Commencement of this Act, or of such Lands as may have been allotted and appropriated for the same Purpose, by or in virtue of any Instruction which may be given by His Majesty, in respect of any Lands granted by His Majesty before the Commencement of this Act, as such Governor, Lieutenant Governor, or Person administering the Government, shall, with the Advice of the said Executive Council, judge to be expedient under the then existing Circumstances of such Township or Parish.

XXXIX. And be it further enacted by the Authority aforesaid, That it shall and may be lawful for His Majesty, His Heirs or Successors, to authorize the Governor, Lieutenant Governor, or Person administering the Government of each of the said Provinces respectively, to present to every such Parsonage or Rectory an Incumbent or Minister of the Church of England, who shall have been duly ordained according to the Rites of the said Church, and to supply from Time to Time such Vacancies as may happen therein; and that every Person so presented to any such Parsonage or Rectory, shall hold and enjoy the same, and all Rights, Profits, and Emoluments thereunto belonging or granted, as fully and amply, and in the same Manner, and on the same Terms and Conditions, and liable to the Performance of the same Duties, as the Incumbent of a Parsonage or Rectory in England.

XL. Provided always, and be it further enacted by the Authority aforesaid, That every such Presentation of an Incumbent or Minister to any such Parsonage or Rectory, and also the Enjoyment of any such Parsonage or Rectory, and of the Rights, Profits, and Emoluments thereof, by any such Incumbent or Minister, shall be subject and liable to all Rights of Institution, and all other Spiritual and Ecclesiastical Jurisdiction and Authority, which have been lawfully granted by His Majesty's Royal Letters Patent to the Bishop of Nova Scotia, or which may hereafter, by His Majesty's Royal Authority, be lawfully granted or appointed to be administered and executed within the said Provinces, or either of them respectively, by the said Bishop of Nova Scotia, or any other Person or Persons, according to the Laws and Canons of the Church of England, which are lawfully made and received in England.

XLI. Provided always, and be it further enacted by the Authority aforesaid, That the several Provisions herein-before contained, respecting the Allotment and Appropriation of Lands for the Support of a Protestant Clergy within the said Provinces, and also respecting the constituting, erecting, and endowing Parsonages and Rectories within the said Provinces, and also respecting the Presentation of Incumbents or Ministers to the same, and also respecting the Manner in which such Incumbents or Ministers shall hold and enjoy the same, shall be subject to be varied or repealed by any express Provisions for that Purpose, contained in any Act or Acts which may be passed by the Legislative Council and Assembly of the said Provinces respectively, and assented to by His Majesty, His Heirs or Successors, under the Restriction herein-after provided.

XLII. Provided nevertheless, and be it further enacted by the Authority aforesaid, That whenever any Act or Acts shall be passed by the Legislative Council and Assembly of either of the said Provinces, containing any Provisions to vary or repeal the above-recited Declaration and Provision contained in the said Act passed in the Fourteenth Year of the Reign of His present Majesty; or to vary or repeal the above-recited Provision contained in His Majesty's Royal Instructions, given on the Third Day of January, in the Year of our Lord One thousand seven-hundred and seventy-five, to the said Guy Carleton Esquire now Lord Dorchester; or to vary or repeal the Provisions herein-before contained for continuing the Force and Effect of the said Declaration and Provisions; or to vary or repeal any of the several Provisions herein-before contained respecting the Allotment and Appropriation of Lands for the Support of a Protestant Clergy within the said Provinces; or respecting the constitution, erecting, or endowing Parsonages or Rectories within the said Provinces; or respecting the Presentation of Incumbents or Ministers to the same; or respecting the Manner in which such Incumbents or Ministers shall hold and enjoy the same: And also that whenever any Act or Acts shall be so passed, containing any Provisions which shall in any Manner relate to or affect the Enjoyment or Exercise of any Religious Form or Mode of Worship; or shall impose or create any Penalties, Burthens, Disabilities, or Disqualifications in respect of the same; or shall in any Manner relate to or affect the Payment, Recovery, or Enjoyment of any of the accustomed Dues or Rights herein-before mentioned; or shall in any Manner relate to the granting, imposing, or recovering any other Dues, or Stipends, or Emoluments whatever, to be paid to or for the Use of any Minister, Priest, Ecclesiastick, or Teacher, according to any Religious Form or Mode of Worship, in respect of his said Office or Function; or shall in any Manner relate to or affect the Establishment or Discipline of the Church of England, amongst the Ministers and Members thereof within the said Provinces; or shall in any Manner relate to or affect the King's Prerogative toughing the granting the Waste Lands of the Crown within the said Provinces; every such Act or Acts shall, previous to any Declaration or Signification of the King's Assent thereto, be laid before both Houses of Parliament in Great Britain; and that it shall not be lawful for His Majesty, His Heirs or Successors, to signify His or their Assent to any such Act or Acts, until Thirty Days after the same shall have been laid before the said Houses, or to assent to any such Act or Acts, in case either House of Parliament shall, within the said Thirty Days, address His Majesty, His Heirs or Successors, to withhold His or their Assent from such Act or Acts; and that no such Act shall be valid or effectual to any of the said Purposes within either of the said Provinces, unless the Legislative Council and Assembly of such Province shall, in the Session in which the same shall have been passed by them, have presented to the Governor, Lieutenant Governor, or Person administering the Government of such Province, an Address or Addresses, specifying that such Act contains Provisions for some of the said Purposes herein-before specially described, and desiring that, in order to give Effect to the same, such Act should be transmitted to England without Delay, for the Purpose of being laid before Parliament previous to the Signification of His Majesty's Assent thereto.

XLIII. And be it further enacted by the Authority aforesaid, That Lands, which shall be heareafter granted within the said Province of Upper Canada shall be granted in Free and Common Soccage, in like Manner as Lands are now holden in Free and Common Soccage, in that Part of Great Britain called England; and that in every Case where Lands shall be hereafter granted within the said Province of Lower Canada, and where the Grantee thereof shall desire the same to be granted in Free and Common Soccage, the same shall be so granted; but subject nevertheless to such Alterations, with respect to the Nature and Consequences of such Tenure of Free and Common Soccage, as may be established by any Law or Laws which may be made by His Majesty, His Heirs or Successors, by and with the Advice and Consent of the Legislative Council and Assembly of the Province.

XLIV. And be it further enacted by the Authority aforesaid, That if any Person or Persons holding any Lands in the said Province of Upper Canada, by virtue of any Certificate of Occupation derive d under the Authority of the Governor and Council of the Province of Quebec, and having Power and Authority to alienate the same, shall at any Time from and after the Commencement of this Act, surrender the same into the Hands of His Majesty, His Heirs or Successors, by Petition to the Governor or Lieutenant Governor, or Person administering the Government of the said Province, setting forth that he, she, or they is or are desirous of holding the same in Free and Common Soccage, such Governor or Lieutenant Governor, or Person administering the Government, shall thereupon cause a fresh Grant to be made to such Person or Persons of such Lands, to be holden in Free and Common Soccage.

XLV. Provided nevertheless, and be it further enacted by the Authority aforesaid, That such Surrender and Grant shall not avoid or bar any Right or Title to any such Lands so surrendered, or any Interest in the same, to which any Person or Persons, other than the Person or Persons surrendering the same, shall have been entitled, either in Possession, Remainder, or Reversion, or otherwise, at the Time of such Surrender; but that every such Surrender and Grant shall be made subject to every such Right, Title, and Interest, and that every such Right, Title or Interest shal be as valid and effectual as if such Surrender and Grant had never been made.

XLVI. And whereas by an Act passed in the Eighteenth Year of the Reign of His present Majesty, intituled, An Act for removing all Doubts and Apprehensions concerning Taxation by the Parliament of Great Britain, in any of the Colonies, Provinces, and Plantations in North America, and the West Indies; and for repealing so much of an Act, made in the Seventh Year of the Reign of His present Majesty, as imposes a Duty on Tea imported from Great Britain into any Colony or Plantation in America, or relates thereto it has been declared, "That the King and Parliament of Great Britain will not impose any Duty, Tax, or Assessment whatever, payable in any of His Majesty's Colonies, Provinces and Plantations in North America or the West Indies, except only such Duties as it may be expedient to impose for the Regulation of Commerce, the Net Produce of such Duties to be always paid and applied to and for the Use of the Colony, Province, or Plantation in which the same shall be respectively levied, in such Manner as other Duties collected by the Authority of the respective General Courts or General Assemblies of such Colonies, Provinces, or Plantations, are ordinarily paid and applied:" And whereas it is necessary, for the general Benefit of the British Empire, that such Power of Regulation of Commerce should continue to be exercised by His Majesty, His Heirs or Successors, and the Parliament of Great Britain, subject nevertheless to the Condition herein-before recited, with respect to the Application of any Duties which may be imposed for that Purpose: Be it therefore enacted by the Authority aforesaid, That nothing in this Act contained shall extend, or be construed to extend, to prevent or affect the Execution of any Law which hath been or shall at any Time be made by His Majesty, His Heirs or Successors, and the Parliament of Great Britain, for establishing Regulations of Prohibitions, or for imposing, levying, or collecting Duties for the Regulation of Navigation, or for the Regulation of the Commerce to be carried on between the said Two Provinces, or between either of the said Provinces and any other Part of His Majesty's Dominions, or between either of the said Provinces and any Foreign Country or State, or for appointing and directing the Payment of Drawbacks of such Duties so imposed, or to give to His Majesty, His Heirs or Successors, any Power or Authority, by and with the Advice and Consent of such Legislative Councils and Assemblies respectively, to vary or repeal any such Law or Laws, or any Part thereof, or in any Manner to prevent or obstruct the Execution thereof.

XLVII. Provided always, and be it enacted by the Authority afore-said, That the Net Produce of all Duties which shall be so imposed shall at all Times hereafter be applied to and for the Use of each of the said Provinces respectively, and in such Manner only as shall be directed by any Law or Laws which may be made by His Majesty, His Heirs or Successors, by and with the Advice and Consent of the Legislative Council and Assembly of such Province.

XLVIII. And whereas, by Reason of the Distance of the said Provinces from this Country, and of the Change to be made by this Act in the Government thereof, it may be necessary that there should be some Interval of Time between the Notification of this Act to the said Provinces respectively, and the Day of its Commencement within the said Provinces respectively: Be it therefore enacted by the Authority aforesaid, That it shall and may be lawful for His Majesty, with the Advice of His Privy Council, to fix and declare, or to authorize the Governor or Lieutenant Governor of the Province of Quebec, or the Person administering the Government there, to fix and declare the Day of the Commencement of this Act within the said Provinces respectively, provided that such Day shall not be later than the Thirty-first Day of December in the Year of our Lord One thousand seven hundred and ninety-one.

XLIX. And be it further enacted by the Authority aforesaid, That the Time to be fixed by His Majesty, His Heirs or Successors, or under his or their Authority, by the Governor, Lieutenant Governor, or Person administering the Government in each of the said Provinces respectively, for issuing the Writs of Summons and Election, and calling together the Legislative Councils and Assemblies of each of the said Provinces respectively, shall not be later than the Thirty-first Day of December in the Year of our Lord One thousand seven hundred and ninety-two.

L. Provided always, and be it further enacted by the Authority afore-said, That during such Interval as may happen between the Commencement of this Act, within the said Provinces respectively, and the First Meeting of the Legislative Council and Assembly of each of the said Provinces respectively, it shall and may be lawful for the Governor or Lieutenant Governor of such Province, or for the Person administering the Government therein, with the Consent of the major Part of such Executive Council as shall be appointed by His Majesty for the Affairs of such Province, to make temporary Laws and Ordinances for the good Government, Peace, and Welfare of such Province, in the same Manner, and under the same Restrictions, as such Laws or Ordinances might have been made by the Council for the Affairs of the Province of Quebec, constituted by virtue of the above-mentioned Act of the Fourteenth Year of the Reign of His present Majesty; and that such temporary Laws or Ordinances shall be valid and binding within such Province, until the Expiration of Six Months after the Legislative Council and Assembly of such Province shall have been first assembled by virtue of and under the Authority of this Act; subject nevertheless to be sooner repealed or varied by any Law or Laws which may be made by His Majesty, His Heirs or Successors, by and with the Advice and Consent of the said Legislative Council and Assembly.

FINIS

THE UNION ACT, 1840, AND SUPPLEMENTARY
ACTS

An Act to re-unite the Provinces of Upper and Lower, Canada, and
for the government of Canada.

23rd July, 1840.

Whereas it is necessary that provision be made for the good government of the Provinces of Upper and Lower Canada, in such manner as may
secure the rights and liberties and promote the interests of all classes of
her Majesty's subjects within the same: And whereas to this end it is expedient that the said Provinces be reunited to form one Province for the
purpose of executive government and legislation: Be it therefore enacted
by the Queen's Most Excellent Majesty, by and with the advice and consent
of the Lords Spiritual and Temporal, and Commons, in the present Parliament assembled, and by the authority of the same, that it shall be lawful
for her Majesty, with the advice of her Privy Council, to declare, or to
authorize the Governor-General of the said two Provinces of Upper and
Lower Canada to declare by proclamation that the said Provinces upon,
from, and after a certain day in such proclamation to be appointed, which
day shall be within fifteen calendar months next after the passing of this
Act, shall form and be one Province under the name of the Province of
Canada, and thenceforth the said Provinces shall constitute and be one Province under the name aforesaid upon, from, and after the day so appointed,
as aforesaid.

II.   And be it enacted that so much of an Act passed in the session of
Parliament held in the thirty-first year of the reign of George the Third,
intituled, "An Act to repeal certain parts of an Act passed in the fourteenth
year of His Majesty's Reign, intituled 'An Act for making more effectual
Provision for the Government of the Province of Quebec in North America,
and to make further Provision for the Government of the said Province,"
as provides for constituting and composing a Legislative Council and Assembly within each of the said Provinces respectively, and for the making
of laws; and also the whole of an Act passed in the session of Parliament
held in the first and second years of the reign of her present Majesty, intituled "An Act to make Temporary Provision for the Government of Lower
Canada;" and also the whole of an Act passed in the session of Parliament
held in the second and third years of the reign of her present Majesty, intituled "An Act to Amend an Act of the las Session of Parliament for making Temporary Provision for the Government of Lower Canada;" and also
the whole of an Act passed in the session of Parliament held in the first
and second years of the reign of his late Majesty King William the Fourth,
intituled "An Act to amend an Act of the fourteenth year of His Majesty,
King George the Third, for establishing a fund towards defraying the
Charges of the Administration of Justice and the Support of Civil Govern-

ment in the Province of Quebec in America;" shall continue and remain in force until the day on which it shall be declared by proclamation, as aforesaid, that the said two Provinces shall constitute and be one Province as aforesaid, and shall be repealed on, from, and after such day: Provided always that the repeal of the said several Acts of Parliament shall not be held to revive or give any force or effect to any enactment which has by the said Acts, or any of them, been repealed or determined.

III.   And be it enacted that from and after the reunion of the said two Provinces there shall be within the Province of Canada one Legislative Council and one Assembly to be severally constituted and composed in the manner herein-after prescribed, which shall be called "The Legislative Council and Assembly of Canada;" and that within the Province of Canada her Majesty shall have power, by and with the advice and consent of the said Legislative Council and Assembly, to make laws for the peace, welfare, and good government of the Province of Canada, such laws not being repugnant to this Act, or to such parts of the said Act passed in the thirty-first year of the reign of his said late Majesty as are not hereby repealed, or to any Act of Parliament made or to be made and not hereby repealed, which does or shall by express enactment or by necessary intendment extend to the Provinces of Upper and Lower Canada, or to either of them, or to the Province of Canada; and that all such laws being passed by the said Legislative Council and Assembly and assented to by her Majesty, or assented to in her Majesty's name by the Governor of the Province of Canada, shall be valid and binding to all intents and purposes within the Province of Canada.

IV.   And be it enacted that for the purpose of composing the Legislative Council of the Province of Canada it shall be lawful for her Majesty, before the time to be appointed for the first meeting of the said Legislative Council and Assembly, by an instrument under the sign manual, to authorize the Governor in her Majesty's name, by an instrument under the Great Seal of the said Province, to summon to the said Legislative Council of the said Province such persons, being not fewer than twenty, as her Majesty shall think fit; and that it shall also be lawful for her Majesty from time to time to authorize the Governor in like manner to summon to the said Legislative Council such other person or persons as her Majesty shall think fit, and that every person who shall be so summoned shall thereby become a member of the Legislative Council of the Province of Canada: Provided always, that no person shall be summoned to the said Legislative Council of the Province of Canada who shall not be of the full age of twenty-one years, and a natural-born subject of her Majesty, or a subject of her Majesty naturalized by Act of the Parliament of Great Britain, or by Act of the Parliament of the United Kingdom of Great Britain and Ireland, or by an Act of the Legislature of either of the Provinces of Upper or Lower Canada, or by an Act of the Legislature of the Province of Canada.

V.   And be it enacted that every member of the Legislative Council of the Province of Canada shall hold his seat therein for the term of his life, but subject nevertheless to the provisions hereinafter contained for vacating the same.

VI.   And be it enacted that it shall be lawful for any member of the Legislative Council of the Province of Canada to resign his seat in the said Legislative Council, and upon such resignation the seat of such Legislative Councillor shall become vacant.

VII.   And be it enacted that if any Legislative Councillor of the Province of Canada shall for two successive sessions of the Legislature of the said Province fail to give his attendance in the said Legislative Council, without the permission of her Majesty or of the Governor of the said Province signified by the said Governor to the Legislative Council, or shall take any oath or make any declaration or acknowledgment of allegiance, obedience,or adherence to any foreign prince or power, or shall do, concur in, or adopt any Act whereby he may become entitled to the rights, privileges, or immunities of a subject or citizen of any foreign state or power, or shall become bankrupt, or take the benefit of any law relating to insolvent debtors, or become a public defaulter, or be attainted of treason, or be convicted of felony or of any infamous crime, his seat in such Council shall thereby become vacant.

VIII.   And be it enacted that any question which shall arise respecting any vacancy in the Legislative Council of the Province of Canada, on occasion of any of the matters aforesaid, shall be referred by the Governor of the Province of Canada to the said Legislative Council, to be by the said Legislative Council heard and determined: Provided always that it shall be lawful, either for the person respecting whose seat such question shall have arisen, or for her Majesty's Attorney-General for the said Province on her Majesty's behalf, to appeal from the determination of the said Council in such case to her Majesty, and that the judgment of her Majesty, given with the advice of her Privy Council thereon, shall be final and conclusive to all intents and purposes.

IX.   And be it enacted that the Governor of the Province of Canada shall have power and authority from time to time, by an instrument under the Great Seal of the said Province, to appoint one member of the said Legislative Council to be Speaker of the said Legislative Council, and to remove him and appoint another in his stead.

X.   And be it enacted that the presence of at least ten member of the said Legislative Council, including the Speaker, shall be necessary to constitute a meeting for the exercise of its powers; and that all questions which shall arise in the said Legislative Council shall be decided by a majority of voices of the members present other than the Speaker, and when the voices shall be equal the Speaker shall have the casting vote.

XI.   And be it enacted that for the purpose of constituting the Legislative Assembly of the Province of Canada it shall be lawful for the Governor of the said Province, within the time hereinafter mentioned and thereafter from time to time as occasion shall require, in her Majesty's name and by an instrument or instruments under the Great Seal of the said Province, to summon and call together a Legislative Assembly in and for the said Province.

XII. And be it enacted that in the Legislative Assembly of the Province of Canada, to be constituted as aforesaid, the parts of the said Province which now constitute the Provinces of Upper and Lower Canada respectively, shall, subject to the provisions hereinafter contained, be represented by an equal number of representatives to be elected for the places and in the manner hereinafter mentioned.

XIII. And be it enacted that the County of Halton in the Province of Upper Canada shall be divided into two ridings, to be called respectively the East Riding and the West Riding; and that the East Riding of the said County shall consit of the following townships, namely; Trafalgar, Nelson, Esquesing, Nassagaweya, East Flamborough, West Flamborough, Ering, Beverly; and that the West Riding of the said County shall consist of the following townships, namely: Garafraxa, Nichol, Woolwich, Guelph, Waterloo, Wilmot, Dumfries, Puslinch, Eramosa; and that the East Riding and West Riding of the said County shall each be represented by one member in the Legislative Assembly of the Province of Canada.

XIV. And be it enacted that the County of Northumberland in the Province of Upper Canada shall be divided into two ridings, to be called respectively the North Riding and the South Riding; and that the North Riding of the last-mentioned County shall consist of the following townships, namely: Monaghan, Otonabee, Asphodel, Smith, Douro, Dummer, Belmont, Methuen, Burleigh, Harvey, Emily, Gore, Ennismore; and that the South Riding of the last-mentioned County shall consist of the following townships, namely: Hamilton, Haldimand, Cramak, Murray, Seymour, Percy; and the North Riding and South Riding of the last-mentioned County shall each be represented by one member in the Legislative Assembly of the Province of Canada.

XV. And be it enacted that the County of Lincoln in the Province of Upper Canada shall be divided into two ridings, to be called respectively the North Riding and the South Riding; and that the North Riding shall be formed by uniting the First Riding and the Second Riding of the said County, and the South Riding by Uniting the Third Riding and Fourth Riding of the said County; and that the North and South Ridings of the last-mentioned County shall each be represented by one member in the Legislative Assembly of the Province of Canada.

XVI. And be it enacted that every county and riding, other than those herein-before specified, which at the time of the passing of this Act was by law entitled to be represented in the Assembly of the Province of Upper Canada, shall be represented by one member in the Legislative Assembly of the Province of Canada.

XVII. And be it eancted that the City of Toronto shall be represented by two members, and the towns of Kingston, Brockville, Hamilton, Cornwall, Niagara, London, and Bytown shall each be represented by one member in the Legislative Assembly of the Province of Canada.

XVIII.   And be it enacted that every county which before and at the time of the passing of the said Act of Parliament, intituled "An Act to make temporary provision for the Government of Lower Canada" was entitled to be represented in the Assembly of the Province of Lower Canada, except the Counties of Montmorency, Orleans, L'Assomption, La Chesnaye, L'Acadie, Laprarie, Dorchester, and Beauce hereinafter mentioned, shall be represented by one member in the Legislative Assembly of the Province of Canada.

XIX.   And be it enacted that the said counties of Montmorency and Orleans shall be united into and form one county to be called the County of Montmorency; and that the said Counties of L"Assomption and La Chesnaye shall be united into and form one county to be called the County of Leinster; and that the said Counties of L"Acadie and Laprairie shall be united into and form one county to be called the County of Huntingdon; and that the Counties of Dorchester and Beauce shall be united into and form one county to be called the County of Dorchester; and that each of the said Counties of Montmorency, Leinster, Huntingdon, and Dorchester shall be represented by one member in the Legislative Assembly of the said Province of Canada.

XX.   And be it enacted that the Cities of Quebec and Montreal shall each be represented by two members, and the Towns of Three Rivers and Sherbrooke shall each be represented by one member in the Legislative Assembly of the Province of Canada.

XXI.   And be it enacted that for the purpose of electing their several representatives to the said Legislative Assembly, the cities and towns hereinbefore mentioned shall be deemed to be bounded and limited in such manner as the Governor of the Province of Canada, by letters patent under the Great Seal of the Province to be issued within thirty days after the union of the said Provinces of Upper Canada and Lower Canada shall set forth and describe; and such parts of any such city or town (if any), which shall not be included within the boundary of such city or town respectively by such letters patent for the purposes of this Act, shall be taken to be a part of the adjoining county or riding for the purpose of being represented in the said Legislative Assembly.

XXII.   And be it enacted that for the purpose of electing the members of the Legislative Assembly of the Province of Canada it shall be lawful for the Governor of the said Province from time to time to nominate proper persons to execute the office of Returning Officer in each of the said counties, ridings, cities, and towns, which shall be represented in the Legislative Assembly of the Province of Canada, subject nevertheless to the provisions hereinafter contained.

XXIII.   And be it enacted that no person shall be obliged to execute the said office of Returning Officer for any longer term than one year, or oftener than once, unless it shall be at any time otherwise provided by some Act or Acts of the Legislature of the Province of Canada

XXIV. And be it enacted that writs for the election of members to serve in the Legislative Assembly of the Province of Canada shall be issued by the Governor of the said Province within fourteen days after the sealing of such instrument, as aforesaid, for summoning and calling together such Legislative Assembly; and that such writs shall be directed to the returning officers of the said counties, ridings, cities, and towns respectively; and that such writs shall be made returnable within fifty days at farthest from the day on which they shall bear date, unless it shall at any time be otherwise provided by any Act of the Legislature of the said Province; and that writs shall in like manner and form be issued for the election of members in the case of any vacancy which shall happen by the death or resignatnion of the person chosen, or by his being summoned to the Legislative Council of the said Province, or from any other legal cause; and that such writs shall be made returnable within fifty days at farthest from the day on which they shall bear date, unless it shall be at any time otherwise provided by any Act of the Legislature of the said Province; and that in any case of any such vacancy which shall happen by the death of the person chosen, or by reason of his being so summoned as aforesaid, the writ for the election of a new member shall be issued within six days after notice thereof shall have been delivered to or left at the office of the proper officer for issuing such writs of election.

XXV. And be it enacted that it shall be lawful for the Governor of the Province of Canada for the time being to fix the time and place of holding elections of members to serve in the Legislative Assembly of the said Province, until otherwise provided for as hereinafter mentioned, giving not less than eight days' notice of such time and place.

XXVI. And be it enacted that it shall be lawful for the Legislature of the Province of Canada, by any Act or Acts to be hereafter passed, to alter the divisions and extent of the several counties, ridings, cities, and towns which shall be represented in the Legislative Assembly of the Province of Canada, and to establish new and other divisions of the same, and to alter the apportionment of representatives to be chosen by the said counties, ridings, cities, and towns respectively, and make a new and different apportionment of the number of representatives to be chosen in and for those parts of the Province of Canada which now constitute the said Provinces of Upper and Lower Canada respectively, and in and for the several districts, counties, ridings, and towns in the same, and to alter and regulate the appointment of returning officers in and for the same, and make provision in such manner as they may deem expedient for the issuing and return of writs for the election of members to serve in the said Legislative Assembly, and the time and place of holding such elections: Provided always that it shall not be lawful to present to the Governor of the Province of Canada for her Majesty's assent any bill of the Legislative Council and Assembly of the said Province by which the number of representatives in the Legislative Assembly may be altered, unless the second and third reading of such bill in the Legislative Council and the

Legislative Assembly shall have been passed with the concurrence of two-thirds of the members for the time being of the said Legislative Assembly respectively, and the assent of her Majesty shall not be given to any such bill unless addresses shall have been presented by the Legislative Council and the Legislative Assembly respectively to the Governor, stating that such bill has been so passed.

XXVII.   And be it enacted that until provisions shall otherwise be made by an Act or Acts of the Legislature of the Province of Canada all the laws which at the time of the passing of this Act are in force in the Province of Upper Canada, and all the laws which at the time of the passing of the said Act of Parliament, intituled "An Act to make temporary provision for the Government of Lower Canada" were in force in the Province of Lower Canada, relating to the qualification and disqualification of any person to be elected, or to sit or vote as a member of the Assembly in the said Provinces respectively, (except those which require a qualification of property in candidates for election, for which provision is hereinafter made), and relating to the qualification and disqualification of voters at the election of members to serve in the Assemblies of the said Provinces respectively, and to the oaths to be taken by any such voters, and to the powers and duties of returning officers, and the proceedings at such elections, and the period during which such elections may be lawfully continued, and relating to the trial of controverted elections and the proceedings incident thereto, and to the vacating of seats of members, and the issuing and execution of new writs in case of any seat being vacated otherwise than by a dissolution of the Assembly, shall respectively be applied to elections of members to serve in the Legislative Assembly of the Province of Canada for places situated in those parts of the Province of Canada for which such laws were passed.

XXVIII.   And be it enacted that no person shall be capable of being elected a member of the Legislative Assembly of the Province of Canada who shall not be legally or equitably seised as of freehold, for his own use and benefit, of lands or tenements held in free and common soccage, or seised or possessed, for his own use and benefit, of lands or tenements h held in fief or in roture, within the said Province of Canada, of the value of five hundred pounds of sterling money of Great Britain, over and above all rents, charges, mortgages, and incumbrances charged upon and due and payable out of or affecting the same; and that every candidate at such election, before he shall be capable of being elected, shall, if required by any other candidate, or by any elector, or by the returning officer, make the following declaration:

"I, A.B., do declare and testify that I am duly seised at law or in equity as of freehold, for my own use and benefit, of lands or tenements held in free and common soccage [or duly seised or possessed for my own benefit, of lands or tenements held in fief or in roture (as the case may be),] in the Province of Canada, of the value of five hundred pounds of sterling money of Great Britain, over and above all rents, mortgages, charges, and incumbrances charged upon, or due and payable out of, or affecting the same; and that I have not collusively or colourably obtained a title to or become possessed of the said lands and tenements, or any part thereof, for the purpose of qualifying or enabling me to be returned a member of the Legislative Assembly of the Province of Canada."

XXIX. And be it enacted that if any person shall knowingly and wilfully make a false declaration respecting his qualification as a candidate at any election as aforesaid, such person shall be deemed to be guilty of a misdemeanor, and being thereof lawfully convicted shall suffer the like pains and penalties as by law are incurred by persons guilty of wilful and corrupt perjury in the place in which such false declaration shall have been made.

XXX. And be it enacted that it shall be lawful for the Governor of the Province of Canada for the time geing to fix such place or places within any part of the Province of Canada, and such times for holding the first and every other session of the Legislative Council and Assembly of the said Province as he may think fit, such times and places to be afterwards changed or varied as the Governor may judge advisable and most consistent with general convenience and the public welfare, giving sufficient notice thereof; and also to prorogue the said Legislative Council and Assembly from time to time, and dissolve the same, by proclamation or otherwise, whenever he shall deem it expedient.

XXXI. And be it enacted that there shall be a session of the Legislative Council and Assembly of the Province of Canada once at least in every year, so that a period of twelve calendar months shall not intervene between the last sitting of the Legislative Council and Assembly in one session and the first sitting of the Legislative Council and Assembly in the next session; and that every Legislative Assembly of the said Province hereafter to be summoned and chosen shall continue for four years from the day of the return of the writs for choosing the same, and no longer, subject nevertheless to be sooner prorogued or dissolved by the Governor of the said Province.

XXXII. And be it enacted that the Legislative Council and Assembly of the Province of Canada shall be called together for the first time at some period not later than six calendar months after the time at which the Provinces of Upper and Lower Canada shall become reunited as aforesaid.

XXXIII. And be it enacted that the members of the Legislative Assembly of the Province of Canada shall, upon the first assembling after every general election, proceed forthwith to elect one of their number to be Speaker; and in case of his death, resignation, or removal by a vote of the said Legislative Assembly, the said members shall forthwith proceed to elect another of such members to be such Speaker; and the Speaker so elected shall preside at all meetings of the said Legislative Assembly.

XXXIV. And be it enacted that the presence of at least twenty members of the Legislative Assembly of the Province of Canada, including the Speaker, shall be necessary to constitute a meeting of the said Legislative

Assembly for the exercise of its powers; and that all questions which shall arise in the said Assembly shall be decided by the majority of voices of such members as shall be present, other than the Speaker, and when the voices shall be equal the Speaker shall have the casting voice.

XXXV. And be it enacted that no member, either of the Legislative Council or of the Legislative Assembly of the Province of Canada, shall be permitted to sit or vote therein until he shall have taken and subscribed the following oath before the Governor of the Said Province, or before some person or persons authorized by such Governor to administer such oath:

"I, A.B., do sincerely promise and swear that I will be faithful and bear true allegiance to her Majesty, Queen Victoria, as lawful Sovereign of the United Kingdom of Great Britain and Ireland, and of this Province of Canada, dependent on and belonging to the said United Kingdom; and that I will defend her to the utmost of my power against all traitorous conspiracies and attempts whatever, which shall be made against her person, crown, and dignity; and that I will do my utmost endeavour to disclose and make known to her Majesty, her heirs and successors, all treasons and traitorous conspiracies and attempts which I shall know to be against her or any of them; and all this I do swear without any equivocation, mental evasion, or secret reservation, and renouncing all pardons and dispensations from any person or persons whatever to the contrary.

SO HELP ME GOD."

XXXVI. And be it enacted that every person authorized by law to make an affirmation instead of taking an oath may make such affirmation in every case in which an oath is hereinbefore required to be taken.

XXXVII. And be it enacted that whenever any bill which has been passed by the Legislative Council and Assembly of the Province of Canada shall be presented for her Majesty's assent to the Governor of the said Province, such Governor shall declare according to his discretion, but subject neverthe less to the provisions contained in this Act, and to such instructions as may from time to time be given in that behalf by her Majesty, her heirs or successors, that he assents to such bill in her Majesty's name, or that he withholds her Majesty's assent, or that he reserves such bill for the signification of her Majesty's pleasure thereon.

XXXVIII. And be it enacted that whenever any bill, which shall have been presented for her Majesty's assent to the Governor of the said Province of Canada, shall by such Governor have been assented to in her Majesty's name, such Governor shall by the first convenient opportunity transmit to one of her Majesty's principal Secretaries of State an authentic copy of such bill so assented to; and that it shall be lawful at any time within two years after such bill shall have been so received by such Secretary of State, for her Majesty by Order in Council to declare her disallowance of such bill; and that such disallowance, together with a certificate under the hand and seal of such Secretary of State certifying the day on which such bill was received as aforesaid, being signified by such Governor to the Legislative Council and Assembly of Canada by speech or message to

the Legislative Council and Assembly of the said Province, or by proclamation, shall make void and annul the same from and after the day of such
signifcation.

XXXIX. And be it enacted that no bill which shall be reserved for
the signification of her Majesty's pleasure thereon shall have any force or
authority within the Province of Canada until the Governor of the said Province shall signify, either by speech or message to the Legislative Council
and Assembly of the said Province, or by proclamation, that such bill has
been laid before her Majesty in Council and that her Majesty has been
pleased to assent to the same; and that an entry shall be made in the journals of the said Legislative Council of every such speech, message, or
proclamation, and a duplicate thereof duly attested shall be delivered to
the proper officer to be kept amongst the records of the said Province; and
that no bill which shall be so reserved as aforesaid shall have any force or
authority in the said Province unless her Majesty's assent thereto shall
have been so signified as aforesaid within the space of two years from the
day on which such bill shall have been presented for her Majesty's assent
to the Governor as aforesaid.

XL. Provided always, and be it enacted that nothing herein contained
shall be construed to limit or restrain the exercise of her Majesty's prerogative in authorizing, and that, notwithstanding this Act and any other
Act or Acts passed in the Parliament of Great Britain, or in the Parliament
of the United Kingdom of Great Britain and Ireland, or of the Legislature
of the Province of Quebec, or of the Provinces of Upper or Lower Canada
respectively, it shall be lawful for her Majesty to authorize the Lieutenant
Governor of the Province of Canada to exercise and execute, within such
parts of the said Province as her Majesty shall think fit, notwithstanding
the presence of the Governor within the Province, such of the powers,
functions, and authority, as well judicial as other, which before and at the
time of passing of this Act were and are vested in the Governor, Lieutenant-Governor, or person administering the Government of the Provinces
of Upper and Lower Canada respectively, or of either of them, and which
from and after the said reunion of the said two Provinces shall become
vested in the Governor of the Province of Canada; and to authorize the Governor of the Province of Canada to assign, depute, substitute, and appoint
any person or persons, jointly or severally, to be his deputy or deputies
within any part or parts of the Province of Canada, and in that capacity to
exercise, perform and execute during the pleasure of the said Governor
such of the powers, functions, and authorities, as well judicial as other,
as before and at the time of the passing of this Act were and are vested in
the Governor, Lieutenant-Governor, or person administering the Government of the Provinces of Upper and Lower Canada respectively, and which
from and after the union of the said Provinces shall become vested in the
Governor of the Province of Canada, as the Governor of the Province of
Canada shall deem to be necessary or expedient: Provided always, that by
the appointment of a deputy or deputies as aforesaid the power and author-

ity of the Governor of the Province of Canada shall not be abridged, altered, or in any way affected otherwise than as her Majesty shall think proper to direct.

XLI. And be it enacted that from and after the said reunion of the said Provinces, all writs, proclamations, instruments for summoning and calling together the Legislative Council and Legislative Assembly of the Province of Canada and for proroguing and dissolving the same, and all writs of summons and election, and all writs and public instruments whatsoever relating to the said Legislative Council and Legislative Assembly or either of them, and all returns to such writs and instruments, and all journals, entries, and written or printed proceedings of what nature soever of the said Legislative Council and Legislative Assembly and each of them respectively, and all written or printed proceedings and reports of committees of the said Legislative Council and Legislative Assembly respectively, shall be in the English language only: Provided always, that this enactment shall not be construed to prevent translated copies of any such documents being made, but no such copy shall be kept among the records of the Legislative Council or Legislative Assembly, or be deemed in any case to have the force of an original record.

XLII. And be it enacted that whenever any bill or bills shall be passed by the Legislative Council and Assembly of the Province of Canada containing any provisions to vary or repeal any of the provisions now in force contained in an Act of the Parliament of Great Britain passed in the fourteenth year of the reign of his late Majesty King George the Third, intituled "An Act for making more effectual provision for the Government of the Province of Quebec in North America," or in the aforesaid Act of Parliament passed in the thirty-first year of the same reign, respecting the accustomed dues and rights of the clergy of the Church of Rome; or to vary or repeal any of the several provisions contained in the said last mentioned Act respecting the allotment and appropriation of lands for the support of the Protestant clergy within the Province of Canada, or respecting the constituting, erecting, or endowing of parsonages or rectories within the Province of Canada, or respecting the presentation of incumbents or ministers of the same, or respecting the tenure on which such incumbents or ministers shall hold or enjoy the same; and also that whenever any bill or bills shall be passed containing any provisions which shall in any manner relate to or affect the enjoyment or exercise of any form or mode of religious worship, or shall impose or create any penalties, burdens, disabilities, or disqualifications in respect of the same, or shall in any manner relate to or affect the payment, recovery, or enjoyment of any of the accustomed dues or rights hereinbefore mentioned, or shall in any manner relate to the granting, imposing, or recovering of any minister, priest, ecclesiastic, or teacher according to any form or mode of religious worship, in respect of his said office or fundtion; or shall in any manner relate to or affect her Majesty's prerogative touching the granting of waste lands of the Crown within the said Province; every such bill or bills shall previously to any declaration or signification of her Majesty's assent thereto, be laid before both Houses of Parliament of the United Kingdom of Great Britain and Ireland; and that it shall not be lawful for her Majesty to signify her assent to any such bill or bills until thirty days after the same shall have been laid before the said Houses, or to assent to any such bill or bills in case either House of Parliament shall within the said thirty days address her Majesty to withhold her assent from any such bill or bills; and that no such bill shall be valid or effectual to any of the said purposes within the said Province of Canada unless the Legislative Council and Assembly of such Province shall in the session in which the same shall have been passed by them, have presented to the Governor of the said Province an address or addresses specifying that such bill or bills contains provisions for some of the purposes hereinbefore specially described, and desiring that, in order to give effect to the same such bill or bills may be transmitted to England without delay, for the purpose of its being laid before Parliament previously to the signification of her Majesty's assent thereto.

XLIII. And whereas by an Act passed in the eighteenth year of the reign of his late Majesty King George the Third, intituled "An Act for removing all Doubts and Apprehensions concerning Taxation by the Parliament of Great Britain in any of the Colonies, Provinces, and Plantations in North America and the West Indies; and for repealing so much of an Act made in the seventh year of the reign of his present Majesty as imposes a duty on Tea imported from Great Britain into any Colony or Plantaltion in America, or relating thereto," it was declared that "the King and Parliament of Great Britain would not impose any duty, tax, or assessment whatever, payable in any of his Majesty's Colonies, Provinces, and Planatations in North America or the West Indies, except only such duties as it might be expedient to impose for the regulation of commerce, the net produce of such duties to be always paid and applied to and for the use of the Colony, Province, or Planatation in which the same shall be respectively levied, in such manner as other duties collected by the authority of the respective General Courts or General Assemblies of such Colonies, Provinces, or Plantations were ordinarily paid and applied": And whereas it is necessary for the general benefit of the Empire that such power of regulation of commerce should continue to be exercised by her Majesty and the Parliament of the United Kingdom of Great Britain and Ireland, subject nevertheless to the conditions hereinbefore recited with respect to the application of any duties which may be imposed for that purpose; be it therefore enacted that nothing in this Act contained shall prevent or affect the execution of any law which hath been or shall be made in the Parliament of the said United Kingdom for establishing regulations and prohibitions, or for the imposing, levying, or collecting duties for the regulation of navigation, or for the regulation of the commerce between the Province of Canada and any other part of her Majesty's Dominions, or between the said Province of Canada or any other part thereof and any foreign country

or state, or for appointing and directing the payment of drawbacks of such
duties so imposed, or to give to her Majesty any power or authority, by
and with the advice and consent of such Legislative Council and Assembly
of the said Province of Canada, to vary or repeal any such law or laws, or
any party thereof, or in any manner to prevent or obstruct the execution
thereof: Provided always, that the net produce of all duties which shall be
so imposed shall at all times hereafter be applied to and for the use of the
said Province of Canada, and (except as hereinafter provided) in such manner only as shall be directed by any laws which may be made by her Majesty, by and with the advice and consent of the Legislative Council and
Assembly of such Province.

XLIV. And whereas by the laws now in force in the said Province
of Upper Canada the Governor, Lieutenant-Governor, or person administering the Government of the said Province, or the Chief Justice of the
said Province, together with any tow or more of the members of the Executive Council of the said Province, constitute and are a Court of Appeal
for hearing and determining all appeals from such judgments or sentences
as may be lawfully brought before them: And whereas by an Act of the
Legislature of the said Province of Upper Canada, passed in the thirty-
third year of the reign of his late Majesty King George the Third, intituled
"An Act to establish a Court of Probate in the said Province, and also a
Surrogate Court in every District thereof," there was and is established
a Court of Probate in the said Province, in which Act it was enacted that
the Governor, Lieutenant-Governor, or person administering the Government of the said last-mentioned Province should preside, and that he
should have the powers and authorities in the said Act specified: And
whereas by an Act of the Legislature of the said Province of Upper Canada,
passed in the second year of the reign of his late Majesty King William the
Fourth, intituled "An Act respecting the Time and Place of Sitting of the
Court of King's Bench," it was amongst other things enacted that his Majesty's Court of King's Bench in that Province should be holden in a place
certain; that is, in the city, town, or place which should be for the time
being the seat of the Civil Government of the said Province, or within one
mile therefrom: And whereas by an Act of the Legislature of the said Province of Upper Canada passed in the seventh year of the reign of his late
Majesty King William the Fourth, intitutled "An Act to Establish a Court
of Chancery in this Province," it was enacted that there should be constituted and established a Court of Chancery to be called and known by the
name and style of "The Court of Chancery for the Province of Upper Canada," of which Court the Governor, Lieutenant-Governor, or person administering the Government of the said Province should be Chancellor;
and which Court, it was also enacted, should be holden at the seat of Government in the said Province, or in such other place as should be appointed by proclamation of the Governor, Lieutenant-Governor, or person administering the Government of the said Province: And whereas by an Act
of the Legislature of the Province of Lower Canada, passed in the thirty-

fourth year of the reign of his late Majesty George the Third, intituled "An Act for the Division of the Province of Lower Canada, for amending the Judicature thereof, and for repealing certain Laws therein mentioned, " it was enacted that the Governor, Lieutenant-Governor, or person administering the Government, the members of the Executive Council of the said Province, the Chief Justice thereof and the Chief Justice to be appointed for the Court of King's Bench at Montreal, or any five of them, the Judges of the Court of the District wherein the judgment appealed from was given excepted, should constitute a Superior Court of Civil Jurisdiction or Provincial Court of Appeals, and should take cognizance of, hear, try, and determine all causes, matters, and things appealed from all civil jurisdictions and Courts wherein an appeal is by law allowed; be it enacted that until otherwise provided by an Act of the Legislature of the Province of Canada, all judicial and ministerial authroity which before and at the time of passing this Act was vested in or might be exercised by the Governor, Lieutenant-Governor, or person administering the Government of the said Province of Upper Canada, or the members or any number of the members of the Executive Council of the same Province, or was vested in or might be exercised by the Governor, Lieutenant-Governor, or the person administering the Government of the Province of Lower Canada, and the members of the Executive Council of that Province, shall be vested in and may be exercised by the Governor, Lieutenant-Governor, or person administering the Government of the Province of Canada, and in the members or hte like number of the members of the Executive Council of the Province of Canada respectively; and that until otherwise provided by Act or Acts of the Legislature of the Province of Canada the said Court of King's Bench, now called the Court of Queen's Bench of Upper Canada, shall from and after the Unio of the Provinces of Upper and Lower Canada be holden at the City of Toronto, or within one mile from the municipal boundary of the said City of Toronto: Provided always, that until otherwise provided by Act or Acts of the Legislature of the Province of Canada, it shall be lawful for the Governor of the Province of Canada, by and with the advice and consent of the Executive Council of the same Province, by his proclamation to fix and appoint such other place as he may think fit, within that part of the last-mentioned Province which now constitutes the Province of Upper Canada, for holding of the said Court of Queen's Bench.

XLV. And be it enacted that all powers, authorities, and functions which by the said Act passed in the thirty-first year of the reign of his late Majesty, King George the Third or by any other Act of Parliament, or by any Act of the Legislature of the Province of Upper and Lower Canada respectively, are vested in or are authorized or required to be exercised by the respective Governors or Lieutenant-Governors of the said Provinces, with the advice or with the advice and consent of the Executive Council of such Provinces respectively, or in conjunction with such Executive Council or with any number of the members thereof, or by the said Governors or Lieutenanty-Governors individually and alone, shall, in so far as the same are not repugnant to or inconsistent with the provisions of this Act, be vested in and may be exercised by the Governor of the Province of Canada, with the advice or with the advice and consent of, or in conjunction as the case may require with such Executive Council, or any members thereof, as may be appointed by her Majesty for the affairs of the Province of Canada, or by the said Governor of the Province of Canada individually and alone in cases when the advice, consent, or concurrence of the Executive Council is not required.

XLVI. And be it enacted that all laws, statues, and ordinances which at the time of the union of the Provinces of Upper and Lower Canada shall be in force within the said Provinces or either of them, or any part of the said Provinces respectively, shall remain and continue to be of the same force, authority, and effect in those parts of the Province of Canada which now constitute the said Provinces respectively as if this Act had not been made, and as if the said two Provinces had not been united as aforesaid, except in so far as the same are repealed or varied by this Act, or in so far as the same shall or may hereafter by virtue and under the authority of this Act be repealed or varied by any Act or Acts of the Legislature of the Province of Canada.

XLVII. And be it enacted that all the courts of civil and criminal jurisdiction within the Provinces of Upper and Lower Canada at the time of the union of the said Provinces and all legal commissions, powers, and authorities, and all officers, judicial, administrative, or ministerial, within the said Provinces respectively, except in so far as the same may be abolished, altered, or varied by or may be inconsistent with the provisions of this Act, or shall be abolished, altered, or varied by any Act or Acts of the Legislature of the Province of Canada, shall contiue to subsist within those parts of the Province of Canada which now constitute the said two Provinces respectively, in the same form and with the same effect as if this Act had not been made, and as if the said two Provinces had not been reunited as aforesaid.

XLVIII. And whereas the Legislatures of the said Provinces of Upper and Lower Canada have from time to time passed enactments, which enactments were to continue in force for a certain number of years after the passing thereof, "and from thence to the end of the then next ensuing session of the Legislature of the Province in which the same were passed;" be it therefore enacted that whenever the words, "and from thence to the end of the then next ensuing session of the Legislature," or words to the same effect, have been used in any temporary Act of either of the said two Provinces which shall not have expired before the reunion of the said two Provinces, the said words shall be construed to extend and apply to the next session of the Legislature of the Province of Canada.

XLIX. And whereas by a certain Act passed in the third year of the reign of his late Majesty, King George the Fourth, intituled, "An Act to regulate the Trade of the Provinces of Upper and Lower Canada, and for other purposes relating to the said Province," certain provisions were

made for appointing arbitrators with power to hear and determine certain
claims of the Province of Upper Canada upon the Province of Lower Canada, and to hear any claim which might be advanced on the part of the Province of Upper Canada to a proportion of certain duties therein mentioned,
and for prescribing the course of proceeding to be pursued by such arbitrators; be it enacted that the said recited provisions of the said last-mentioned Act, and all matters in the same Act contained, which are conse-
quent to or dependent upon the said provisions or any of them, shall be repealed.

L. And be it enacted that upon the union of the Provinces of Upper
and Lower Canada, all duties and revenues over which the respective Legislatures of the said Provinces before and at the time of the passing of
this Act had and have power of appropriation, shall form one consolidated
revenue fund to be appropriated for the public service of the Province of
Canada in the manner and subject to the charges hereinafter mentioned.

LI. And be it enacted that the said consolidated revenue fund of the
Province of Canada shall be permanently charged with all the costs,
charges, and expences incident to the collection, management, and receipt thereof, such costs, charges and expences, being subject nevertheless to be reviewed and audited in such manner as shall be directed by any
Act of the Legislature of the Province of Canada.

LII. And be it enacted that out of the consolidated revenue fund of
the Province of Canada there shall be payable in every year to her Majesty,
her heirs and successors, the sum of forty-five thousand pounds for defraying the expence of the several serices and purposes named in the
Schedule marked A, to this Act annexed; and during the life of her Majesty,
there shall be payable to her Majesty, her heirs and successors, out of
the said consolidated revenue fund, a further sum of thirty thousand
pounds, for defraying the expence of the several services and purposes
named in the Schedule marked B to the Act annexed; the said sums of
forty-five thousand pounds and thirty thousand pounds to be issued by the
Receiver-General in discharge of such warrant or warrants as shall be
from time to time directed to him under the hand and seal of the Governor;
and the said Receiver-General shall account to her Majesty for the same,
through the Lord High Treasurer or Lords Commissioners of her Majesty'
Treasury, in such form and manner as her Majesty shall be graciously
pleased to direct.

LIII. And be it enacted that, until altered by any Act of the Legislature of the Province of Canada, the salaries of the Governor and of the
Judges shall be those respectively set against their several offices in the
said Schedule A.; but that it shall be lawful for the Governor to abolish
any of the offices named in the said Schedule B.; or to vary the sums appropriated to any of the services or purposes named in the said Schedule
B.; and that the amount of saving which may accrue from any such alteration in either of the said schedules shall be appropriated to such purposes
connected with the administration of the Government of the said Provinces

as to her Majesty shall seem fit; and that accounts in detail of the expenditure of the several sums of forty-five thousand and thirty thousand pounds hereinbefore granted, and of every part thereof, shall be laid before the Legislative Council and Legislative Assembly of the said Province within thirty days next after the beginning of the session after such expenditure shall have been made: Provided always that not more than two thousand pounds shall be payable at the same time for pensions to the judges out of the said sum of forty-five thousand pounds, and that not more than five thousand pounds shall be payable at the same time for pensions out of the said sum of thirty thousand pounds; and that a list of all such pensions and of the persons to whom the same shall have been granted, shall be laid in every year before the said Legislative Council and Legislative Assembly.

LIV. And be it enacted that during the time for which the said several sums of forty-five thousand pounds and thirty thousand pounds are severally payable the same shall be accepted and taken by her Majesty by way of Civil List, instead of all territorial and other revenues now at the disposal of the Crown, arising in either of the said Provinces of Upper Canada or Lower Canada, or in the Province of Canada, and that three-fifths of the net produce of the said territorial and other revenues now at the disposal of the Crown within the Province of Canada shall be paid over to the account of the said consolidated revenue fund; and also during the life of her Majesty and for five years after the demise of her Majesty the remaining two-fifths of the net produce of the said territorial and other revenues and at the disposal of the Crown within the Province of Canada shall be also paid over in like manner to the account of the said consolidated revenue fund.

LV. And be it enacted that the consolidation of the duties and revenues of the said Province shall not be taken to affect the payment out of the said consolidated revenue fund of any sum or sums heretofore charged upon the rates and duties already raised, levied, and collected to and for the use of either of the said Provinces of Upper Canada or Lower Canada, or of the Province of Canada, for such time as shall have been appointed by the several Acts of the Legislature of the Province by which such charges were severally authorized.

LVI. And be it enacted that the expences of the collection, management, and receipt of the said consolidated revenue fund shall form the first charge thereon; and that the annual interest of the Public Debt of the Provinces of Upper and Lower Canada, or of either of them, at the time of the reunion of the said Provinces shall form the second charge thereon; and that the payments to be made to the clergy of the United Church of England and Ireland, and to clergy of the Church of Scotland, and to ministers of other Christian denominations, pursuant to any law or usage whereby such payments before or at the passing of this Act were or are legally or usually paid out of the public or Crown revenue of either of the Provinces of Upper and Lower Canada, shall form the third charge upon the said consolidated revenue fund; and that the said sum of forty-five

thousand pounds shall form the fourth charge thereon; and that the said
sum of thirty thousand pounds, so long as the same shall continue to be
payable, shall form the fifth charge thereon; and that the other charges
upon the rates and duties levied within the said Province of Canada herein-
before reserved shall form the sixth charge thereon, so long as such
charges shall continue to be payable.

LVII. And be it enacted that, subject to the several payments hereby charged on the said Consolidated Revenue Fund, the same shall be appropriated by the Legislature of the Province of Canada for the public service in such manner as they shall think proper: Provided always that all
bills for appropriating any part of the surplus of the said consolidated revenue fund, or for imposing any new tax or import, shall originate in the
Legislative Assembly of the said Province of Canada: Provided also that it
shall not be lawful for the said Legislative Assembly to originate or pass
any vote, resolution, or bill for the appropriation of any part of the surplus of the said consolidated revenue fund, or of any other tax or impost,
to any purpose which shall not have been first recommended by a message
of the Governor to the said Legislative Assembly during the session in
which such vote, resolution, or bill shall be passed.

LVIII. And be it enacted that it shall be lawful for the Governor, by
an instrument or instruments to be issued by him for that purpose under
the Great Seal of the Province to constitute townships in those parts of the
Province of Canada in which townships are not already constituted, and to
fix metes and bounds thereof, and to provide for the election and appointment of township officers therein, who shall have and exercise the like
powers as are exercised by the like officers in the townships already constituted in that part of the Province of Canada now called Upper Canada;
and every such instrument shall be published by proclamation, and shall
have the force of law from a day to be named in each case in such proclamation.

LIX. And be it enacted that all powers and authorities expressed in
this Act to be given to the Governor of the Province of Canada shall be exercised by such Governor in conformity with and subject to such orders,
instructions, and directions as her Majesty shall from time to time see
fit to make or issue.

LX. And whereas his late Majesty King George the Third, by his
Royal Proclamation bearing date the seventh day of October in the third
year of his reign, was pleased to declare that he had put the coast of Labrador from the River St. John to Hudson's Straits, with the islands of
Anticosti and Madelaine and all other smaller islands lying on the said
coast, under the care and inspection of the Governor of Newfoundland;
And whereas by an Act passed in the fourteenth year of the reign of his
said late Majesty, intituled "An Act for making more effectual provision
for the Government of the Province of Quebec in North America," all such
territories, islands, and countries, which had since the tenth day of Feb-

ruary in the year one thousand seven hundred and sixty-three been made part of the Government of Newfoundland, were during his Majesty's pleasure annexed to and made part and parcel of the Province of Quebec as created and established by the said proclamation; be it hereby declared and enacted that nothing in this or any other Act contained shall be construed to restrain her Majesty, if she shall be so pleased, from annexing the Magdalen Islands in the Gulf of St. Lawrence to her Majesty's Island of Prince Edward.

LXI. And be it enacted that in this Act, unless otherwise expressed therein, the words "Act of the Legislature of the Province of Canada" are to be understood to mean "Act of her Majesty, her Heirs or Successors, enacted by her Majesty, or by the Governor on behalf of her Majesty, with t the advice and consent of the Legislative Council and Assembly of the Province of Canada"; and the words "Governor of the Province of Canada" are to be understood as comprehending the Governor, Lieutenant-Governor, or person authorized to execute the Office or the functions of Governor of the said Province.

LXII. And be it enacted that this Act may be amended or repealed by any Act to be passed in the present session of Parliament.

SCHEDULES.

SCHEDULE A.

Governor	£ 7000
Lieutenant-Governor	1000

Upper Canada.

1 Chief Justice	1500
4 Puisne Judges, at £900 each	3600
1 Vice-Chancellor	1125

Lower Canada.

1 Chief Justice, Quebec	1500
3 Puisne Judges, Quebec, at £900 each	2700
1 Chief Justice, Montreal	1100
3 Puisne Judges, Montreal, at £900 each	2700
1 Resident Judge at Three Rivers	900
1 Judge of the Inferior Distric of St. Francis	500
1 Judge of the Inferior Distric of Gaspe	500
Pensions to the Judges, salaries of the Attornies and Solicitors General, and contingent and miscellaneous expences of Administration of Justice throughout the Province of Canada	20875
	£ 45000

SCHEDULE B.

Civil Secretaries and their Offices	£ 8000
Provincial Secretaries and their Offices	3000
Receiver-General and his Office	3000
Inspector-General and his Office	2000
Executive Council	3000
Board of Works	2000
Emigrant Agent	700
Pensions	5000
Contingent Expences of Public Offices	3300
	£30000

DOCUMENTS CONCERNING CONFEDERATION

Introduction

The following transcription of the Quebec Conference Resolutions (October 10, 1864) and the final form of the British North America Act of 1867, represent the collective wishes of the individual colonies involved and Britain's attempt to accomodate these wishes. The Quebec Resolutions have been reproduced many times as has the British North America Act. There is however, only one extant copy of the Quebec Resolutions of any authority. This copy, now in the possession of the Ontario Department of Public Records and Archives, carries the signatures of John A. Macdonald and G. E. Cartier. (A facsimile reproduction of this document is in the possession of the Public Archives of Canada in Ottawa.)

This document was the result of the second of three conferences. The first or Charlottetown Conference had been called to discuss the union of the Maritime Provinces and Canada had sent representatives to "observe". The Canadian representatives managed to convince the conference of the possibility of a wider union than the one being discussed and consequently the Quebec Conference was assembled. After this second conference, representatives were sent to England with their proposals as set out in the Quebec Resolutions. On December 6, 1866 at the suggestion of the Colonial Office, a third conference was held. The result of this last conference was summarized in the London Resolutions (December 24, 1866). The differences between the London Resolutions and the Quebec Resolutions are slight.

The British North America Act has been amended several times since it was promulgated on July 1, 1867. Although this is essentially the constitution of Canada, any amendment pertaining to federal and provincial powers must still be passed through the British Parliament. The reasons for this political anachronism are varied but chiefly it is because agreement cannot be reached between the provincial and federal authorities as to the transference of the Act into the Canadian Statutes without jeapardizing their respective positions within the constitution.

Quebec Resolutions

Report of Resolutions adopted at aConference of Delegates from the Provinces of Canada, Nova Scotia and New Brunswick, and the Colonies of Newfoundland and Prince Edward Island, held at the city of Quebec, October 10, 1864, as the Basis of a proposed Confederation of those Provinces and Colonies.

1. The best interests and present and future prosperity of British North America will be promoted by a Federal Union under the Crown of Great Britian, provided such Union can be effected on principles just to the several Provinces.

2. In the Federation of the British North American Provinces the system of government best adapted under existing circumstances to protect the diversified interests of the several Provinces, and secure efficiency, harmony, and permanency in the working of the Union, -- would be a General Government charged with matters of common interest to the whole country, and Local Governments for each of the Canadas and for the Provinces of Nova Scotia, New Brunswick, and Prince Edward Island, charged with the control of local matters in their respective sections, provision being made for the admission into the Union on equitable terms of Newfoundland, the Northwest Territory, British Columbia, and Vancouver.

3. In framing a Constitution for the General Government, the Conference, with a view to the perpetuation of our connexion with the Mother Country, and to the promotion of the best interests of the people of these Provinces, desire to follow the model of the British Constitution, so far as our circumstances will permit.

4. The Executive Authority or Government shall be vested in the Sovereign of the United Kingdom of Great Britian and Ireland, and be administered according to the well understood principles of the British Constitution by the Sovereign personally or by the Representative of the Sovereign duly authorized.

5. The Sovereign or Representative of the Sovereign shall be Commander-in-Chief of the Land and Naval Militia Forces.

6. There shall be a general Legislature or Parliament for the Federated Provinces, composed of a Legislative Council and a House of Commons.

7. For the purpose of forming the Legislative Council, the Federated Provinces shall be considered as consisting of three divisions: -- 1st, Upper Canada; 2nd, Lower Canada; 3rd, Nova Scotia, New Brunswick, and Prince Edward Island; each division with an equal representation in the Legislative Council.

8. Upper Canada shall be represented in the Legislative Council by 24 members, Lower Canada by 24 members, and the three Maritime Provinces by 24 members, of which Nova Scotia shall have 10, New Brunswick 10, and Prince Edward Island four members.

9. The Colony of Newfoundland shall be entitled to enter the proposed Union, with a representation in the Legislative Council of four members.

10. The Northwest Territory, British Columbia, and Vancouver shall be admitted into the Union, on such terms and conditions as the Parliament of the Federated Provinces shall deem equitable, and as shall receive the assent of Her Majesty; and in the case of the Province of British Columbia or Vancouver, as shall be agreed to by the Legislature of such Province.

11. The Members of the Legislative Council shall be appointed by the Crown under the Great Seal of the General Government, and shall hold office during life; if any Legislative Councillor shall, for two consecutive sessions of Parliament, fail to give his attendance in the said Council, his seat shall thereby become vacant.

12. The Members of the Legislative Council shall be British subjects by birth or naturalization, of the full age of 30 years, shall possess a continuous real property qualification of four thousand dollars over and above all incumbrances, and shall be and continue worth that sum over and above their debts and liabilities, but in the case of Newfoundland an Prince Edward Island the property may be either real or personal.

13. If any question shall arise as to the qualification of a Legislative Councillor, the same shall be determined by the Council.

14. The first selection of the Members of the Legislative Council shall be made, except as regards Prince Edward Island, from the Legislative Councils of the various Provinces, so far as a sufficient number be found qualified and willing to serve. Such Members shall be appointed by the Crown at the recommendation of the General Executive Government, upon the nomination of the respective Local Governments; and in such nomination due regard shall be had to the claims of the Members of the Legislative Council of the opposition in each Province, so that all political parties may as nearly as possible be fairly represented.

15. The Speaker of the Legislative Council (unless otherwise provided by Parliament) shall be appointed by the Crown from among the Members of the Legislative Council, and shall hold office during pleasure, and shall only be entitled to a casting vote on an equality of votes.

16. Each of the 24 Legislative Councillors representing Lower Canada in the Legislative Council of the General Legislature shall be appointed to represent one of the 24 electoral divisions mentioned in Schedule A of Chapter 1st of the Consolidated Statutes of Canada, and such Councillor shall reside or possess his qualification in the division he is appointed to represent.

17. The basis of Representation in the House of Commons shall be population, as determined by the official census every 10 years; and the number of Members at first shall be 194, distributed as follows:

Upper Canada 82
Lower Canada 65
Nova Scotia 19
New Brunswick 15
Newfoundland 8
and Prince Edward Island 5

18. Until the official census of 1871 has been made up, there shall be no change in the number of Representatives from the several sections.

19. Immediately after the completion of the census of 1871, and immediately after every decennial census thereafter, the representation from each section in the House of Commons shall be re-adjusted on the basis of population.

20. For the purpose of such re-adjustments, Lower Canada shall always be assigned 65 Members, and each of the other sections shall at each re-adjustment receive for the 10 years then next succeeding, the number of Members to which it will be entitled on the same ratio of representation to population as Lower Canada will enjoy according to the census last taken by having 65 Members.

21. No reduction shall be made in the number of Members returned by any section unless its population shall have decreased relatively to the population of the whole Union to the extent of five per centum.

22. In computing at each decennial period the number of Members to which each section is entitled, no fractional parts shall be considered unless when exceeding one-half the number entitling to a Member, in which case a Member shall be given for each such fractional part.

23. The Legislature of each Province shall divide such Province into the proper number of constituencies, and define the boundaries of each of them.

24. The Local Legislature of each Province may, from time to time, alter the electoral districts for the purposes of representation in the House of Commons, and distribute the Representatives to which the Province is entitled, in any manner such Legislature may think fit.

25. The number of Members may at any time be increased by the General Parliament, regard being had to the proportionate rights then existing.

26. Until provisions are made by the General Parliament all the laws which at the date of the Proclamation constituting the Union are in force in the Provinces respectively relating to the qualification and disqualification of any person to be elected or to sit or vote as a Member of the Assembly in the said Provinces respectively--and relating to the qualification or disqualification of voters, and to the oaths to be taken by voters, and to Returning Officers and their powers and duties--and relating to the proceedings at elections,--and to the period during which such elections may be continued,--and relating to the trial of controverted elections, and the proceedings incident thereto, --and relating to the vacating of seats of Members,--and the issuing and execution of new writs in case of any seat being vacated otherwise than by a dissolution,--shall respectively apply to elections of Members to serve in the House of Commons, for places situate in those Provinces respectively.

27. Every House of Commons shall continue for five years from the day of the return of the writs choosing the same, and no longer, subject, nevertheless, to be sooner prorogued or dissolved by the Governor.

28. There shall be a Session of the General Parliament once at least in every year, so that a period of 12 calendar months shall not intervene between the last sitting of the General Parliament in one session and the first sitting thereof in the next session.

29. The General Parliament shall have power to make Laws for the peace, welfare and good Government of the Federated Provinces (saving the Sovereignty of England), and especially Laws respecting the following subjects:

1. The public debt and property.
2. The regulation of trade and commerce.
3. The imposition or regulation of duties of customs on imports and exports, except on exports of timber, logs, masts, spaars, deals, and sawn lumber, and of coal and other minerals.
4. The imposition and regulation of excise duties.
5. The raising of money by all or any other modes or systems of taxation.
6. The borrowing of money on the public credit.
7. Postal service.
8. Lines of steam or other ships, railways, cwnals and other works, connecting any two or more of the Provinces together, or extending beyond the limits of any Province.
9. Lines of steamships between the Federated Provinces and other countries.
10. Telegraphic communication and the incorporation of telegraph companies.
11. All such works as shall, although lying wholly within any Province, be specially declared by the Acts authorizing them to be for the general advantage.
12. The census.
13. Militia--Military and naval service and defence.
14. Beacons, buoys, and lighthouses.
15. Navigation and shipping.
16. Quarantine.
17. Sea coast and inland fisheries.
18. Ferries between any Province and a foreign country, or between any two Provinces.
19. Currency and coinage.
20. Banking, incorporation of banks, and the issue of paper money.
21. Saving banks.
22. Weights and measures.
23. Bills of exchange and promissory notes.
24. Interest.
25. Legal tender.
26. Bankruptcy and insolvency.
27. Patents of invention and discovery.
28. Copyrights.
29. Indians and lands reserved for the Indians.
30. Naturalization and aliens.
31. Marriage and divorce.
32. The criminal law, excepting the constitution of Courts of criminal jurisdiction, but including the procedure in criminal matters.
33. Rendering uniform all or any of the laws relative to property

and civil rights in Upper Canada, Nova Scotia, New Brunswick, Newfoundland, and Prince Edward Island, and rendering uniform the procedure of all or any of the Courts in these Provinces; but any Statute for this purpose shall have no force or authority in any Province until canctioned by the Legislature thereof.

34. The establishment of a General Court of Appeal for the Federated Provinces.

35. Immigration.

36. Agriculture.

37. And generally respecting all matters of a general character, not specially and exclusively reserved for the Local Governments and Legislatures.

30. The General Government and Parliament shall have all powers necessary or proper for performing the obligations of the Federated Provinces, as part of the British Empire, to Foreign Countries, arising under Treaties between Great Britain and such Countries.

31. The General Parliament may also from time to time establish additional Courts, and the General Government may appoint Judges and Officers thereof, when the same shall appear necessary or for the public advantage, in order to the due execution of the Laws of Parliament.

32. All Courts, Judges, and Officers of several Provinces shall aid, assist, and obey the General Government in the exercise of its rights and powers, and for such purposes shall be held to be Courts, Judges, and Officers of the General Government.

33. The General Government shall appoint and pay the Judges of the Superior Courts in each Province and of the County Courts of Upper Canada, and Parliament shall fix their salaries.

34. Until the Consolidation of the Laws of Upper Canada, New Brunswick, Nova Scotia, Newfoundland, and Prince Edward Island, the Judges of these Provinces appointed by the General Government shall be selected from their respective Bars.

35. The Judges of the Courts of Lower Canada shall be selected from the Bar of Lower Canada.

36. The Judges of the Court of Admiralty now receiving salaries shall be paid by the General Government.

37. The Judges of the Superior Courts shall hold their offices during good behaviour, and shall be removable only on the Address of both Houses of Parliament.

Local Government

38. For each of the Provinces there shall be an Executive Officer, styled the Lieutenant-Governor, who shall be appointed by the Governor General in Council, under the Great Seal of the Federated Provinces, during pleasure; such pleasure not to be exercised before the expiration of the first five years, except for cause, such cause to be communicated in writing to the Lieutenant-Governor immediately after the exercise of the pleasure as aforesaid, and also by Messages to both Houses of Parliament, within the first week of the first session afterwards.

39. The Lieutenant-Governor of each Province shall be paid by the General Government.

40. In undertaking to pay the salaries of the Lieutenant-Governors, the Conference does not desire to prejudice the claim of Prince Edward Island upon the Imperial Government for the amount now paid for the salary of the Lieutenant-Governor thereof.

41. The Local Government and Legislature of each Province shall be constructed in such manner as the existing Legislature of such Province shall provide.

42. The Local Legislature shall have power to alter or amend their Constitution from time to time.

43. The Local Legislatures shall have power to make Laws respecting the following subjects:

1. Direct taxation and the imposition of duties on the export of timber, logs, masts, spars, deals, and sawn lumber, and of coals and other minerals.

2. Borrowing money on the credit of the Province.

3. The establishment and tenure of local offices, and the appointment and payment of local officers.

4. Agriculture.

5. Immigration.

6. Education; saving the rights and privileges which the Protestant or Catholic minority in both Canadas may possess as to their denominational schools at the time when the Union goes into operation.

7. The sale and management of public lands, excepting lands belonging to the General Government.

8. Sea coast and inland fisheries.

9. The establishment, maintenance, and management of penitentiaries, and of public and reformatory prisons.

10. The establishment, maintenance, and management of hospitals, asylums, charities, an eleemosynary institutions.

11. Municipal institutions.

12. Shop, saloon, tavern, auctioneer, and other licences.

13. Local works.

14. The incorporation of private or local companies, except such as relate to matters assigned to the General Parliament.

15. Property and civil rights, excepting those portions thereof assigned to the General Parliament.

16. Inflicting punishment by fine, penalties, imprisonment, or otherwise for the breach of laws passed in relation to any subject within their jurisdiction.

17. The administration of justice, including the constitution, maintenance, and organization of the courts, both of civil and criminal jurisdiction, and including also the Procedure in civil matters.

18. And generally all matters of a private or local nature, not assigned to the General Parliament.

44. The power of respiting, reprieving, and pardoning prisoners convicted of crimes, and of commuting and remitting of sentences in whole or in part, which belongs of right to the Crown, shall be administered by the Lieutenant-Governor of each Province in Council, subject

to any instructions he may from time to time receive from the General Government, and subject to any provisions that may be made in this behalf by the General Parliament.

Miscellaneous

45. In regard to all subjects over which jurisdiction belongs to both the General and Local Legislatures, the laws of the General Parliament shall control and supersede those made by the Local Legislature, and the latter shall be void as far as they are repugnant to or inconsistent with the former.

46. Both the English and French languages may be employed in the General Parliament and in its proceedings, and in the Local Legislature of Lower Canada, and also in the Federal Courts and in the Courts of Lower Canada.

47. No lands or property belonging to the General or Local Government shall be liable to taxation.

48. All bills for appropriating any part of the public revenue, or for imposing any new tax or impost, shall originate in the House of Commons or the House of Assembly, as the case may be.

49. The House of Commons or House of Assembly shall not originate or pass any vote, resolution, address, or bill for the appropriation of any part of the public revenue, or of any tax or impost to any purpose, not first recommended by Message of the Governor-General or the Lieutenant-Governor, as the case may be, during the session in which such vote, resolution, address, or bill is passed.

50. Any bill of the General Parliament may be reserved in the usual manner for Her Majesty's assent, and any bill of the Local Legislatures may in like manner be reserved for the consideration of the Governor-General.

51. Any bill passed by the General Parliament shall be subject to disallowance by Her Majesty within two years, as in the case of bills passed by the Legislatures of the said Provinces hitherto, and in like manner any bill passed by a Local Legislature shall be subject to disallowance by the Governor-General within one year after the passing thereof.

52. The seat of Government of the Federated Provinces shall be Ottawa, subject to the Royal Prerogative.

53. Subject to any future action of the respective Local Governments, the seat of the Local Government in Upper Canada shall be Toronto; of Lower Canada, Quebec; and the seats of the Local Governments in the other Provinces shall be as at present.

Property and Liabilities

54. All stocks, cash bankers' balances, and securities for money belonging to each Province at the time of the Union, except as hereinafter mentioned, shall belong to the General Government.

55. The following public works and property of each Province shall belong to the Geneal Government, to wit:

1. Canals;
2. Public harbours;
3. Lighthouses and piers;
4. Steamboats, dredges, and public vessels;

5. River and lake improvements;
6. Railway and railway stocks, mortgages, and other debts due by railway companies;
7. Military roads;
8. Customhouses, post offices, and other public buildings, except such as may be set aside by the General Government for the use of the Local Legislature and Governments;
9. Property transferred by the Imperial Government, and known as Ordnance property;
10. Armouries, drill sheds, military clothing, and munitions of war; and
11. Lands set apart for public purposes.

56. All lands, mines, minerals, and royalties vested in Her Majesty in the Provinces of Upper Canada, Lower Canada, Nova Scotia, New Brunswick, and Prince Edward Island, for the use of such Provinces, shall belong to the Local Government of the territory in which the same are so situate; subject to any trusts that may exist in respect to any of such lands or to any interest of other persons in respect of the same.

57. All sums due from purchasers or lessees of such lands, mines, or minerals at the time of the Union shall also belong to the Local Governments.

58. All assets connected with such portions of the public debt of any Province as are assumed by the Local Governments shall also belong to those Governments respectively.

59. The several Provinces shall retain all other public property therein subject to the right of the General Government to assume any lands or public property required for fortifications or the defence of the country.

60. The General Government shall assume all the debts and liabilities of each Province.

61. The debt of Canada not specially assumed by Upper and Lower Canada respectively, shall not exceed at the time of the Union $62,500,000; Nova Scotia shall enter the Union with a debt not exceeding $8,000,000; and New Brunswick with a debt not exceeding $7,000,000.

62. In case Nova Scotia or New Brunswick do not incur liabilities beyond those for which their Governments are now bound, and which shall make their debts at the date of Union less than $8,000,000 and $7,000,000 respectively, they shall be entitled to interest at 5 per cent on the amount not so incurred, in like manner as hereinafter provided for Newfoundland Prince Edward Island; the foregoing Resolution being in no respect intended to limit the powers given to the respective Governments of those Provinces by legislative authority, but only to limit the maximum amount of charge to be assumed by the General Government. Provided always, that the powers so conferred by the respective Legislatures shall be exercised within five years from this date, or the same shall then lapse.

63. Newfoundland and Prince Edward Island, not having incurred debts equal to those of the other Provinces, shall be entitled to receive by half-yearly payments in advance from the General Government the interest at five per cent on the difference between the actual amount of their respective debts at the time of the Union, and the average amount

of indebtedness per head of the population of Canada, Nova Scotia, and New Brunswick.

64. In consideration of the transfer to the General Parliament of the powers of taxation, an annual grant in aid of each Province shall be made, equal to 80 cents per head of the population, as established by the census of 1861, the population of Newfoundland being estimated at 130,000. Such aid shall be in full settlement of all future demands upon the General Government for local purposes, and shall be paid half-yearly in advance to each Province.

65. The position of New Brunswick being such as to entail large immediate charges upon her local revenues, it is agreed that for the period of 10 years from the time when the Union takes effect an additional allowance of $63,000 per annum shall be made to that Province. But so long as the liability of that Province remains under $7,000,000, a deduction equal to the interest on such deficiency shall be made from the $63,000.

66. In consideration of the surrender to the General Government by Newfoundland of all its rights in mines and minerals, and of all the ungranted and unoccupied lands of the Crown, it is agreed that the sum of $150,000 shall each year be paid to that Province, by semi-annual payments. Provided that that Colony shall retain the right of opening, constructing, and controlling roads and bridges through any of the said lands, subject to any laws which the General Parliament may pass in respect of the same.

67. All engagements that may before the Union be entered into with the Imperial Government for the defence of the country shall be assumed by the General Government.

68. The General Government shall secure without delay the completion of the Intercolonial Railway from Rivière-du-Loup through New Brunswick to Truro in Nova Scotia.

69. The communications with the Northwestern Territory and the improvements required for the development of the trade of the Great West with the Seaboard, are regarded by this Conference as subjects of the highest importance to the Federated Provinces, and shall be prosecuted at the earliest possible period that the state of the finances will permit.

70. The sanction of the Imperial and Local Parliaments shall be sought for the Union of the Provinces, on the principles adopted by the Conference.

71. That Her Majesty the Queen be solicited to determine the rank and name of the Federated Provinces.

72. The proceedings of the Conference shall be authenticated by the signatures of the Delegates, and submitted by each Delegation to its own Government, and the Chairman is authorized to submit a copy to the Governor General for transmission to the Secretary of State for the Colonies.

I certify that the above is a true copy of the original Report of Resolutions adopted in Conference.

E. P. Taché
Chairman.

The British North America Act, 1867

An Act for the Union of Canada, Nova Scotia, and New Brunswick, and the Government thereof; and for purposes connected therewith.

29th March, 1867.

Whereas the Provinces of Canada, Nova Scotia, and New Brunswick have expressed their Desire to be federally united into One Dominion under the Crown of the United Kingdom of Great Britain and Ireland, with a Constitution similar in Principle to that of the United Kingdom:

And whereas such a Union would conduce to the Welfare of the Provinces and promote the Interests of the British Empire:

And whereas on the Establishment of Union by Authority of Parliament it is expedient, not only that the Constitution of the Legislative Authority in the Dominion be provided for, but also that the Nature of the Executive Government therein be declared:

And whereas it is expedient that Provision be made for the eventual admission into the Union of other Parts of British North America:

Be it therefore enacted and declared by the Queen's most Excellent Majesty, by and with the Advice and Consent of the Lords Spiritual and Temporal, and Commons, in this present Parliament assembled, and by the Authority of the same, as follows:

I. PRELIMINARY

1. This Act may be cited as the British North America Act 1867.

2. The Provisions of this Act referring to Her Majesty the Queen extend also to the Heirs and Successors of Her Majesty, Kings and Queens of the United Kingdom of Great Britain and Ireland.

II. UNION

3. It shall be lawful for the Queen, by and with the Advice of Her Majesty's Most Honourable Privy Council, to declare by Proclamation that, on and after a Day therein appointed, not being more than Six Months after the passing of this Act, the Provinces of Canada, Nova Scotia, and New Brunswick shall form and be One Dominion under the Name of Canada; and on and after that Day those Three Provinces shall form and be One Dominion under that Name accordingly.

4. The subsequent Provisions of this Act shall, unless it is otherwise expressed or implied, commence and have effect on and after the Union, that is to say, on and after the Day appointed for the Union taking effect in the Queen's Proclamation; and in the same Provisions, unless it is otherwise expressed or implied, the Name Canada shall be taken to mean Canada as constituted under the Act.

5. Canada shall be divided into Four Provinces, named Ontario, Quebec, Nova Scotia, and New Brunswick.

6. The Parts of the Province of Canada (as it exists at the passing of this Act) which formerly constituted respectively the Provinces of

Upper Canada and Lower Canada shall be deemed to be severed, and shall form two separate Provinces. The Part which formerly constituted the Province of Upper Canada shall constitute the Province of Ontario; and the Part which formerly constituted the Province of Lower Canada shall constitute the Province of Quebec.

7. The Provinces of Nova Scotia and New Brunswick shall have the same limits as at the passing of this Act.

8. In the General Census of the Population of Canada which is hereby required to be taken in the Year One Thousand eight hundred and seventy-one, and in every Tenth Year thereafter, the respective Populations of the Four Provinces shall be distinguished.

III. EXECUTIVE POWER

9. The Executive Government and Authority of and over Canada is hereby declared to continue and be vested in the Queen.

10. The Provisions of this Act referring to the Governor General extend and apply to the Governor General for the Time being of Canada, or other the Chief Executive Officer or Administrator for the Time being carrying on the Government of Canada on behalf and in the Name of the Queen, by whatever Title he is designated.

11. There shall be a Council to aid and advise in the Government of Canada, to be styled the Queen's Privy Countil for Canada; and the Persons who are to be Members of that Council shall be from Time to Time chosen and summoned by the Governor General and sworn in as Privy Councillors, and Members thereof may be from Time to Time removed by the Governor General.

12. All Powers, Authorities, and Functions which under any Act of the Parliament of Great Britain, or of the Parliament of the United Kingdom of Great Britain and Ireland, or of the Legislature of Upper Canada, Lower Canada, Nova Scotia, or New Brunswick, are at the Union vested in or exercisable by the respective Governors or Lieutenant-Governors of those Provinces, with the advice, or with the Advice and Consent, of the respective Executive Councils thereof, or in conjunction with those Councils, or with any Number of Members thereof, or by those Governors or Lieutenant-Governors individually, shall, as far as the same continue in existence and capable of being exercised after the Union in relation to the Government of Canada, be vested in and ex-erciseable by the Governor General, with the Advice or with the Advice and Consent of or in conjunction with the Queen's Privy Council for Canada, or any Members thereof, or by the Governor General individually, as the Case requires, subject nevertheless (except with respect to such as exist under Acts of the Parliament of Great Britain or of the Par-liament of the United Kingdom of Great Britain and Ireland) to be abolished or altered by the Parliament of Canada.

13. The Provisions of this Act referring to the Governor General in Council shall be construed as referring to the Governor General acting by and with the Advice of the Queen's Privy Council for Canada.

14. It shall be lawful for the Queen, if Her Majesty thinks it fit, to authorize the Governor General from Time to Time to appoint any Person or any Persons jointly or severally to be his Deputy or Deputies within any Part or Parts of Canada, and in that Capacity to exercise during

the Pleasure of the Governor General such of the Powers, Authorities, and Functions of the Governor General deems it necessary or expedient to assign to him or them, subject to any Limitations or Directions expressed or given by the Queen; but the Appointment of such a Deputy or Deputies shall no affect the Exercise by the Governor General himself of any Power, Authority, or Function.

15. The Commander-in-Chief of the Land and Naval Militia, and of all Naval and Military Forces, of and in Canada, is hereby declared to continue and be vested in the Queen.

16. Until the Queen otherwise directs the seat of Government of Canada shall be Ottawa.

IV. LEGISLATIVE POWER

17. There shall be One Parliament for Canada, consisting of the Queen, an Upper House styled the Senate, and the House of Commons.

18. The Privileges, Immunities, and Powers to be held, enjoyed and exercised by the Senate and by the House of Commons and by the Members thereof respectively shall be such as are from Time to Time defined by Act of the Parliament of Canada, but so that the same shall never exceed those at the passing of this Act held, enjoyed, and exercised by the Commons House of Parliament of the United Kingdom of Great Britain and Ireland and by the Members thereof.

19. The Parliament of Canada shall be called together not later than six Months after the Union.

20. There shall be a Session of the Parliament of Canada once at least in every Year, so that Twelve Months shall not intervene between the last Sitting of the Parliament in one Session and its first Sitting in the next Session.

The Senate

21. The Senate shall, subject to the Provisions of this Act, consist of Seventy-two Members, who shall be styled Senators.

22. In relation to the Constitution of the Senate, Canada shall be deemed to consist of Three Divisions;

1. Ontario;

2. Quebec;

3. The Maritime Provinces, Nova Scotia and New Brunswick; which Three Divisions shall (subject to the Provisions of this Act) be equally represented in the Senate as follows: Ontario by Twenty-four Senators; Quebec by Twenty-four Senators; and the Maritime Provinces by Twenty-four Senators, Twelve thereof representing New Brunswick.

In the case of Quebec each of the Twenty-four Senators representing that Province shall be appointed for One of the Twenty-four Electoral Divisions of Lower Canada specified in Schedule A. to Chapter One of the Consolidated Statutes of Canada.

23. The Qualification of a Senator shall be as follows:

1. He shall be of the full age of Thirty Years:

2. He shall be either a Natural-born Subject of the Queen, or a Subject of the Queen naturalized by an Act of the Parliament of Great Britain, or of the Parliament of the United Kingdom of Great Britain and Ireland, or of the Legislature of One of the

Provinces of Upper Canada, Lower Canada, Canada, Nova Scotia, or New Brunswick, before the Union, or of the Parliament of Canada, after the Union:

3. He shall be legally or equitably seised as of Freehold for his own Use and Benefit of Lands or Tenements held in free and common Socage, or seised or possessed for his own Use and Benefit of Lands or Tenements held in Franc-alleu or in Roture, within the Province for which he is appointed, of the Value of Four thousand Dollars, over and above all Rents, Dues, Debts, Charges, Mortgages, and Incumbances due or payable out of or charged on or affecting the same:

4. His Real and Personal Property shall be together worth Four thousand Dollars over and above his Debts and Liabilities:

5. He shall be resident in the Province for which he is appointed:

6. In the case of Quebec he shall have his Real Property Qualification in the Electoral Division for which he is appointed, or shall be resident in that Division.

24. The Governor General shall from Time to Time in the Queen's Name, by Instrument under the Great Seal of Canada, summon qualified Persons to the Senate; and, subject to the Provisions of this Act, every Person so summoned shall become and be a Member of the Senate and a Senator.

25. Such Persons shall be first summoned to the Senate as the Queen by Warrant under Her Majesty's Royal Sign Manual thinks fit to approve, and their Names shall be inserted in the Queen's proclamation of Union.

26. If at any Time on the Recommendation of the Governor General the Queen thinks fit to direct that Three or Six Members be added to the Senate, the Governor General may by Summons to Three or Six qualified Persons (as the Case may be), representing equally the Three Divisions of Canada, add to the Senate accordingly.

27. In case of such Addition being at any Time made the Governor General shall not summon any Person ot the Senate, except on a further like Direction by the Queen on the like Recommendation, until each of the Three Divisions of Canada is represented by Twenty-four Senators and no more.

28. The Number of Senators shall not at any Time exceed Seventy-eight.

29. A Senator shall, subject to the Provisions of this Act, hold his Place in the Senate for Life.

30. A Senator may by Writing under his Hand addressed to the Governor General resign his Place in the Senate, and thereupon the same shall be vacant.

31. The Place of a Senator shall become vacant in any of the following cases:

1. If for Two consecutive Sessions of the Parliament he fails to give his Attendance in the Senate.

2. If he takes an Oath or makes a Declaration or Acknowledgement of Allegiance, Obedience, or Adherence to a Foreign Power, or does an Act whereby he becomes a Subject or Citizen, or entitled to the Rights or Privileges of a Subject or Citizen,

of a Foreign Power:

3. If he is adjudged Bankrupt or Insolvent, or applies for the Benefit of any Law relating to Insolvent Debtors, or becomes a Public Defaulter:

4. If he is attainted of Treason or convicted of Felony or of any infamous Crime:

5. If he ceases to be qualified in respect of Property or of Residence; provided, that a Senator shall not be deemed to have ceased to be qualified in respect of Residence by reason only of his residing at the Seat of the Government of Canada while holding an Office under that Government requiring his Presence there.

32. When a Vacancy happens in the Senate by Resignation, Death, or otherwise, the Governor General shall by Summons to a fit and qualified Person fill the Vacancy.

33. If any Question arises respecting the Qualification of a Senator or a Vacancy in the Senate the same shall be heard and determined by the Senate.

34. The Governor General may from Time to Time, by instrument under the Great Seal of Canada, appoint another in his Stead.

35. Until the Parliament of Canada otherwise provides, the Presence of at least Fifteen Senators, including the Speaker, shall be necessary to constitute a Meeting of the Senate for the Exercise of its Powers.

36. Questions arising in the Senate shall be decided by a Majority of Voices, and the Speaker shall in all Cases have a Vote, and when the Voices are equal the Decision shall be deemed to be in the Negative.

The House of Commons

37. The House of Commons shall, subject to the Provisions of this Act, consist of One hundred and eighty-one Members, of whom Eighty-two shall be elected for Ontario, Sixty-five for Quebec, Nineteen for Nova Scotia, and Fifteen for New Brunswick.

38. The Governor General shall from Time to Time, in the Queen's Name, by Instrument under the Great Seal of Canada, summon and call together the House of Commons.

39. A Senator shall not be capable of being elected or of sitting or voting as a Member of the House of Commons.

40. Until the Parliament of Canada otherwise provides, Ontario, Quebec, Nova Scotia, and New Brunswick shall, for the Purposes of the Election of Members to serve in the House of Commons, be divided into Electoral Districts as follows:

1. Ontario

Ontario shall be divided into the Counties, Ridings of Counties, Cities, Parts of Cities, and Towns enumerated in the First Schedule to this Act, each whereof shall be an Electoral District, each such District as numbered in that Schedule being entitled to return One Member.

2. Quebec

Quebec shall be divided into Sixty-five Electoral Districts, composed of the Sixty-five Electoral Divisions into which Lower Canada is at the passing of this Act divided under Chapter Two of the Consolidated Statutes of Canada, Chapter Seventy-five of the Consolidated Statutes for Lower Canada, and the Act of the Province of Canada of the Twenty-third Year of the Queen, Chapter One, or any other Act amending the same in force at the Union, so that each such Electoral Division shall be for the Purposes of this Act an Electoral District entitled to return One Member.

3. Nova Scotia

Each of the Eighteen Counties of Nova Scotia shall be an Electoral District. The County of Halifax shall be entitled to return Two Members, and each of the other Counties One Member.

4. New Brunswick

Each of the Fourteen Counties into which New Brunswick is divided, including the City and County of St. John, shall be an Electoral District. The City of St. John shall also be a separate Electoral District. Each of those Fifteen Electoral Districts shall be entitled to return One Member.

41. Until the Parliament of Canada otherwise provides, all Laws in force in the several Provinces at the Union relative to the following Matters or any of them, namely--the Qualifications and Disqualifications of Persons to be elected or to sit or vote as Members of the House of Assembly or Legislative Assembly in the several Provinces, the Voters at Elections of such Members, the Oaths to be taken by Voters, the Returning Officers, their Powers and Duties, the Proceedings at Elections, the Periods during which Elections may be continued, the Trial of Controverted Elections, and Proceedings incident thereto, the vacating of Seats of Members, and the Execution of new Writs in case of Seats vacated otherwise than by Dissolution, -- shall respectively apply to Elections of Members to serve in the House of Commons for the same several Provinces.

Provided that, until the Parliament of Canada otherwise provides, at any Election for a Member of the House of Commons for the District of Algoma, in addition to Persons qualified by the Law of the Province of Canada to vote, every male British Subject, aged Twenty-one Years or upwards, being a Householder, shall have a Vote.

42. For the First Election of Members to serve in the House of Commons the Governor General shall cause Writs to be issued by such Person, in such Form and addressed to such Returning Officers as he thinks fit.

The Person issuing writs under this Section shall have the like Powers as are possessed at the Union by the Officers charged with the issuing of Writs for the Election of Members to serve in the respective House of Assembly or Legislative Assembly of the Province of Canada, Nova Scotia, or New Brunswick; and the Returning Officers to whom Writs are directed under this Section shall have the like Powers as are possessed at the Union by the Officers charged with the returning of Writs for the Election of Members to serve in the same respective House of Assembly or Legislative Assembly.

43. In case a Vacancy in the Representation in the House of Commons or any Electoral District happens before the Meeting of the Parliament, or after the Meeting of the Parliament before Provision is made by the Parliament in this Behalf, the Provisions of the last foregoing

Section on this Act shall extend and apply to the issuing and returning of a Writ in respect of such Vacant District.

44. The House of Commons on its first assembling after a General Election shall proceed with all practicable Speed to elect One of its Members to be Speaker.

45. In case of a Vacancy happening in the Office of Speaker by Death, Resignation, or otheriwise, the House of Commons shall with all practicable Speed proceed to elect another of its Members to be Speaker.

46. The Speaker shall preside at all Meetings of the House of Commons.

47. Until the Parliament of Canada otherwise provides, in case of the Absence for any Reason of the Speaker from the Chair of the House of Commons for a period of Forty-eight consecutive Hours, the House may elect another of its Members to act as Speaker, and the Member so elected shall during the Continuance of such Absence of the Speaker have and execute all the Powers, Privileges, and Duties of Speaker.

48. The presence of at least Twenty Members of the House of Commons shall be necessary to constitute a Meeting of the House for the Exercise of its Powers; and for that Purpose the Speaker shall be reckoned as a Member.

49. Questions arising in the House of Commons shall be decided by a Majority of Voices other than that of the Speaker, and when the Voices are equal, but not otherwise, the Speaker shall have a Vote.

50. Every House of Commons shall continue for Five Years from the Day of the Return of the Writs for choosing the House (subject to be sooner disolved by the Governor General), and no longer.

51. On the Completion of the Census in the Year One Thousand Eight hundred and seventy-one, and of each subsequent decennial Census, the Representation of the Four Provinces shall be readjusted by such Authority, in such manner, and from such Time, as the Parliament of Canada from Time to Time provides, subject and according to the following rules:

1. Quebec shall have the fixed Number of Sixty-five Members:

2. There shall be assigned to each of the other Provinces such such a Number of Members as will bear the same Proportion to the Number of tis Population (ascertained at such Census) as the Number Sixty-five bears to the Number of the Population of Quebec (so ascertained):

3. In the Computation of the Number of Members for a Province a fractional Part not exceeding One Half the whole Number requisite for entitling the Province to a Member shall be disregarded; but a fractional Part exceeding One Half of that Number shall be equivalent to the whole Number:

4. On any such Re-adjustment the Number of Members for a Province shall not be reduced unless the Proportion which the Number of the Population of the Province bore to the Number of the aggregate Population of Canada at the then last preeceding Re-adjustment of the Number of Members for the Province is ascertained at the then latest Census to be diminished by One Twentieth Part or upwards:

5. Such Re-adjustment shall not take effect until the Termination

of the then existing Parliament.

52. The Number of Members of the House of Commons may be from Time to Time increased by the Parliament of Canada, provided the proportionate Representation of the Province prescribed by this Act is not thereby disturbed.

Money Votes; Royal Assent

53. Bills for appropriating any Part of the Public Revenue, or for imposing any Tax or Impost, shall originate in the House of Commons.

54. It shall not be lawful for the House of Commons to adopt or pass any Vote, Resolution, Address, or Bill for the Appropriation of any Part of the Public Revenue, or of any Tax or Impost, to any Purpose that has not been first recommended to the House by Message of the Governor General in the Session in which such Vote, Resolution, Address, or Bill is proposed.

55. Where a Bill passed by the Houses of Parliament is presented to the Governor General for the Queen's Assent, he shall declare, according to his Discretion, but subject to the Provisions of this Act and to Her Majesty's Instructions, either that he assents thereto in the Queen's Name, or that he withholds the Queen's Assent, or that he reserves the Bill for the Signification of the Queen's Pleasure.

56. Where the Governor General assents to a Bill in the Queen's Name, he shall by the first convenient Opportunity send an authentic Copy of the Act to one of Her Majesty's Principal Secretaries of State, and if the Queen in Council within Two Years after Receipt thereof by the Secretary of State thinks fit to disallow the Act, such Disallowance (with a Certificate of the Secretary of State of the Day on which the Act was received by him) being signified by the Governor General, by Speech or Message to each of the Houses of the Parliament or by Proclamation, shall annul the Act from and after the Day of such Signification.

57. A Bill reserved for the Signification of the Queen's Pleasure shall not have any force unless and until within Two Years from the Day on which it was presented to the Governor General for the Queen's Assent, the Governor General signifies, by Speech or Message to each of the Houses of the Parliament or by Proclamation, that it has received the Assent of the Queen in Council.

An Entry of every such Speech, Message, or Proclamation shall be made in the Journal of each House, and a Duplicate thereof duly attested shall be delivered to the proper Officer to be kept among the Records of Canada.

V. PROVINCIAL CONSTITUTION
Executive Power

58. For each Province there shall be an Officer, styled the Lieutenant-Governor, appointed by the Governor General in Council by Instrument under the Great Seal of Canada.

59. A Lieutenant-Governor shall hold Office during the Pleasure of the Governor General; but any Lieutenant-Governor appointed after the Commencement of the First Session of the Parliament of Canada shall not be removable within Five Years from his Appointment, except for Cause assigned, which shall be communicated to him in Writing within One Month after the Order for his Removal is made, and shall be com-

municated by Message to the Senate and to the House of Commons within One Week thereafter if the Parliament is then sitting, and if not then within One Week after the Commencement of the next Session of the Parliament.

60. The Salaries of the Lieutenant-Governors shall be fixed and provided by the Parliament of Canada.

61. Every Lieutenant-Governor shall, before assuming the Duties of his Office, make and subscribe before the Governor General or some Person authorized by him, Oaths of Allegiance and Office similar to those taken by the Governor General.

62. The Provisions of this Act referring to the Lieutenant-Governor extend and apply to the Lieutent-Governor for the Time being of each Province or other the Chief Executive Officer of Administrator for the Time being carrying on the Government of the Province, by whatever Title he is designated.

63. The Executive Council of Ontario and of Quebec shall be composed of such Persons as the Lieutenant-Governor from Time to Time thinks fit, and in the first instance of the following Officers, namely-- the Attorney-General, the Secretary and Registrar of the Province, the Treasurer of the Province, the Commissioner of Crown Lands, and the Commissioner of Agriculture and Public Works, within Quebec, the Speaker of the Legislative Council and the Solicitor General.

64. The Constitution of the Executive Authority in each of the Provinces of Nova Scotia and New Brunswick shall, subject to the Provisions of this Act, continue as it exists at the Union until altered under the Authority of this Act.

65. All Powers, Authorities, and Functions which under any Act of the Parliament of Great Britain, or of the Parliament of the United Kingdom of Great Britain and Ireland, or of the Legislature of Upper Canada, Lower Canada, or Canada, were or are before or at the Union vested in or exercisable by the respective Governors or Lieutenant-Governors of those Provinces, with the Advice or with the Advice and Consent of the respective Executive Councils thereof, or in conjunction with those Councils, or with any Number of Members thereof, or by those Governors or Lieutenant-Governors individually, shall, as far as the same are capable of being exercised after the Union in relation to the Government of Ontario and Quebec respectively, be vested in and shall or may be exercised by the Lieutenant-Governor of Ontario and Quebec respectively, with the Advice or with the Advice and Consent of or in conjunction with the respective Executive Councils, or any Members thereof or by the Lieutenant-Governor individually, as the Case requires, subject nevertheless (except with respect to such as exist under Acts of the Parliament of Great Britain, or of the Parliament of the United Kingdom of Great Britain and Ireland,) to be abolished or altered by the respective Legislatures of Ontario and Quebec.

66. The Provisions of this Act referring to the Lieutenant-Governor in Council shall be construed as referring to the Lieutenant-Governor of the Province acting by and with the Advice of the Executive Council thereof.

67. The Governor General in Council may from Time to Time appoint

an Administrator to execute the Office and Functions of Lieutenant-Governor during his Absence, Illness, or other Inability.

68. Unless and until the Executive Government of any Province otherwise directs with respect to that Province, the Seats of Government of the Provinces shall be as follows, namely,--of Ontario, the City of Toronto; of Quebec, the City of Quebec; of Nova Scotia, the City of Halifax; and of New Brunswick, the City of Fredericton.

Legislative Power

1. Ontario

69. There shall be a Legislature for Ontario consisting of the Lieutenant-Governor and of One House, styled the Legislative Assembly of Ontario.

70. The Legislative Assembly of Ontario shall be composed of Eighty-two Members, to be elected to represent the Eighty-two Electoral Districts set forth in the First Schedule to this Act.

2. Quebec

71. There shall be a Legislature for Quebec consisting of the Lieutenant-Governor and of Two Houses, styled the Legislative Council of Quebec and the Legislative Assembly of Quebec.

72. The Legislative Council of Quebec shall be composed of Twenty-four Members, to be appointed by the Lieutenant-Governor, in the Queen's name, by Instrument under the Great Seal of Quebec, one being appointed to represent each of the Twenty-four Electoral Divisions of Lower Canada in this Act referred to, and each holding Office for the Term of his Life, unless the Legislature of Quebec otherwise provides under the Provisions of this Act.

73. Qualifications of the Legislative Councillors of Quebec shall be the same as those of the Senators for Quebec.

74. The Place of a Legislative Councillor of Quebec shall become vacant in the Cases, mutatis mutandis in which the Place of Senator becomes vacant.

75. When a vacancy happens in the Legislative Council of Quebec by Resignation, Death, or otherwise, the Lieutenant-Governor, in the Queen's Name, by Instrument under the Great Seal of Quebec, shall appoint a fit and qualified Person to fill the Vacancy.

76. If any Question arises respecting the Qualification of a Legislative Councillor of Quebec, or a Vacancy in the Legislative Council of Quebec, the same shall be heard and determined by the Legislative Council.

77. The Lieutenant-Governor may from Time to Time, by Instrument under the Great Seal of Quebec, appoint a Member of the Legislative Council of Quebec to be Speaker thereof, and may remove him and appoint another in his stead.

78. Until the Legislature of Quebec otherwise provides, the Presence of at least Ten Members of the Legislative Council, including the Speaker, shall be necessary to constitute a Meeting for the Exercise of its Powers.

79. Questions arising in the Legislative Council of Quebec shall be decided by a Majority of Voices, and the Speaker shall in all Cases have

a Vote, and when the Voices are equal the Decision shall be deemed to be in the negative.

80. The Legislative Assembly of Quebec shall be composed of Sixty-five Members, to be elected to represent the Sixty-five Electoral Divisions or Districts of Lower Canada in this Act referred to, subject to Alteration thereof by the Legislature of Quebec: Provided that it shall not be lawful to present to the Lieutenant-Governor of Quebec for Assent any Bill for altering the Limits of any of the Electoral Divisions or Districts mentioned in the Second Schedule to this Act, unless the Second and Third Readings of such Bill have been passed in the Legislative Assembly with the Concurrence of the Majority of the Members representing all those Electoral Divisions or Districts, and the Assent shall not be given to such Bill unless an Address has been presented by the Legislative Assembly to the Lieutenant-Governor stating that it has been so passed.

3. Ontario and Quebec

81. The Legislatures of Ontario and Quebec respectively shall be called together not later than Six Months after the Union.

82. The Lieutenant-Governor of Ontario and of Quebec shall from Time to Time, in the Queen's Name, by Instrument under the Great Seal of the Provinces, summon and call together the Legislative Assembly of the Province.

83. Until the Legislature of Ontario or of Quebec otherwise provides, a Person accepting or holding in Ontario or in Quebec any Office, Commission, or Employment, permanent or temporary, at the Nomination of the Lieutenant-Governor, to which an annual Salary, or any Fee, Allowance Emolument, or profit of any Kind or Amount whatever from the Province is attached, shall not be eligible as a Member of the Legislative Assembly of the respective Province, nor shall he sit or vote as such; but nothing in this Section shall make ineligible any Person being a Member of the Executive Council of the respective Province, or holding any of the following Offices, that is to say, the Offices of the Attorney-General, Secretary and Registrar of the Province, Treasurer of the Province, Commissioner of Crown Lands, and Commissioner of Agriculture and Public Works, and in Quebec Solicitor General, or shall disqualify him to sit or vote in the House for which he is elected, provided he is elected while holding such Office.

84. Until the Legislatures of Ontario and Quebec respectively otherwise provide, all Laws which at the Union are in force in those Provinces respectively, relative to the following Matters, or any of them, namely,-- the Qualifications and Disqualifications of Persons to be elected or to sit or vote as Members of the Assembly of Canada, the Qualifications or Disqualifications of Voters, the Oaths to be taken by Voters, the Returning Officers, their Powers and Duties, the Proceedings at Elections, the Periods during which such Elections may be continued, and the Trial of controverted Elections and the Proceedings incident thereto, the vacating of the Seats of Members and the issuing and Execution of new Writs in case of Seats vacated otherwise than by Dissolution,--shall respectively

apply to Elections of Members to serve in the respective Legislative Assemblies of Ontario and Quebec.

Provided that until the Legislature of Ontario otherwise provides, at any Election for a Member of the Legislative Assembly of Ontario for the District of Algoma, in addition to Persons qualified by the Law of the Province of Canada to vote, every male British Subject, aged Twenty-one Years or upwards, being a Householder, shall have a vote.

85. Every Legislative Assembly of Ontario and every Legislative Assembly of Quebec shall continue for Four Years from the Day of the Return of the Writs for choosing the same (subject nevertheless to either the Legislative Assembly of Ontario or the Legislative Assembly of Quebec being sooner dissolved by the Lieutenant-Governor of the Province), and no longer.

86. There shall be a session of Legislature of Ontario and of that of Quebec once at least in every Year, so that Twelve Months shall not intervene between the last Sitting of the Legislature in each Province in one Session and its first Sitting in the next Session.

87. The following Provisions of this Act respecting the House of Commons of Canada shall extend and apply to the Legislative Assemblies of Ontario and Quebec, that is to say--the Provisions relating to the Election of a Speaker originally and on Vacancies, the Duties of the Speaker, the absence of the Speaker, the Quorum, and the Mode of voting, as if those Provisions were here re-enacted and made applicable in Terms to each such Legislative Assembly.

4. Nova Scotia and New Brunswick

88. The Constitution of the Legislature of each of the Provinces of Nova Scotia and New Brunswick shall, subject to the provisions of this Act, continue as it exists at the Union altered under the Authority of this Act, and the House of Assembly of New Brunswick existing at the passage of this Act shall, unless sooner dissolved, continue for the Period for which it was elected.

5. Ontario, Quebec, and Nova Scotia

89. Each of the Lieutenant-Governors of Ontario, Quebec and Nova Scotia shall cause Writs to be issued for the First Election of Members of the Legislative Assembly thereof in such Form and by such Person as he thinks fit, and at such Time and addressed to such Returning Officer as the Governor General directs, and to that the First Election of a Member of the Assembly for any Electoral District or any Subdivision thereof shall be held at the same Time and at the same Place as the Election for a Member to serve in the House of Commons of Canada for that Electoral District.

6. The Four Provinces

90. The following Provisions of this Act respecting the Parliament of Canada, namely--the Provisions relating to Appropriation and Tax Bills, the Recommendation of Money Votes, the Assent to Bills, the Disallowance of Acts, and the Signification of Pleasure on Bills reserved,-- shall extend and apply to the Legislatures of the several Provinces as if

those Provisions were here re-enacted and made applicable in Terms to the respective Provinces and the Legislatures thereof, with the Substitution of the Lieutenant-Governor of the Province for the Governor General, of the Governor General for the Queen and for a Secretary of State, of One Year for Two Years, and of the Province of Canada.

VI. DISTRIBUTION OF LEGISLATIVE POWERS

Powers of Parliament

91. It shall be lawful for the Queen by and with the Advice and Consent of the Senate and House of Commons, to make Laws for the Peace, Order and good Government of Canada, in relation to all Matters not coming within the Classes of Subjects by this Act assigned exclusively to the Legislatures of the Provinces; and for greater Certainty, but not so as to restrict the Generality of the foregoing Terms of this Section, it is hereby declared that (notwithstanding anything in this Act) the exclusive Authority of the Parliament of Canada exaends to all Matters coming within the Classes of Subjects next hereinafter enumerated; that is to say--

1. The Public Debt and Property.
2. The Regulation of Trade and Commerce.
3. The raising of Money by any Mode or System of Taxation.
4. The borrowing of Money on the Public Credit.
5. Postal Service.
6. The Census and Statistics.
7. Militia, Military and Naval Service, and Defence.
8. The fixing of and providing for the Salaries and Allowances of Civil and other Officers of the Government of Canada.
9. Beacons, Buoys, Lighthouses, and Sable Island.
10. Navigation and Shipping.
11. Quarantine and the Establishment and Maintenance of Marine Hospitals.
12. Sea Coast and Inland Fisheries.
13. Ferries between a Province and any British or Foreign Country or between Two Provinces.
14. Currency and Coinage.
15. Banking, Incorporation of Banks, and the Issue of Paper Money. Money.
16. Savings Banks.
17. Weights and Measures.
18. Bills of Exchange and Promissory Notes.
19. Interest.
20. Legal Tender.
21. Bankruptcy and Insolvency.
22. Patents of Invention and Discovery.
23. Copyrights.
24. Indians, and Lands reserved for the Indians.
25. Naturalization and Aliens.
26. Marriage and Divorce.
27. The Criminal Law, except the Constitution of Courts of

Criminal Jurisdiction, but including the Procedure in Criminal Matters.

28. The Establishment, Maintenance, and Management of Penitentiaries.

29. Such Classes of Subjects as are expressly excepted in the Enumeration of the Classes of Subjects by this Act assigned exclusively to the Legislature of the Provinces.

And any Matter coming within any of the Classes of Subjects enumerated in this Section shall not be deemed to come within the Class of Matters of a local or private Nature comprised in the Enumeration of the Classes of Subjects by this Act assigned exclusively to the Legislatures of the Provinces.

Exclusive Powers of Provincial Legislatures

92.   In each Province the Legislature may exclusively make Laws in relation to Matters coming within the Classes of Subjects next hereinafter enumerated; that is to say, --

1. The Amendment from Time to Time, notwithstanding anything in this Act, of the Constitution of the Province, except as regards the Office of Lieutenant-Governor.

2. Direct Taxation within the Province in order to the Raising of a Revenue for Provincial Purposes.

3. The borrowing of Money on the sole Credit of the Province.

4. The Establishment and Tenure of Provincial Offices and the Appointment and Payment of Provincial Officers.

5. The Management and Sale of the Public Lands belonging to the Province and of the Timber and Wood thereon.

6. The Establishment, Maintenance, and Management of Public and Reformatory Prisons in and for the Province.

7. The Establishment, Maintenance, and Management of Hospitals, Asylums, Charities, and Eleemosynary Institutions in and for the Province, other than Marine Hospitals.

8. Municipal Institutions in the Province.

9. Shop, Saloon, Tavern, Auctioneer, and other Licenses in order to the raising of a Revenue for Provincial, Local, or Municipal Purposes.

10. Local Works and Undertakings other than such as are of the following Classes:

(a) Lines of Steam or other Ships, Railways, Canals, Telegraphs, and other Works and Undertakings connecting the Province with any other or others of the Provinces, or extending beyond the Limits of the Province:

(b) Lines of Steams Ships between the Province and any British or Foreign Country:

(c) Such Works as, although wholly situate within the Province, are before or after their Execution declared by the Parliament of Canada to be for the general Advantage of Canada or for the Advantage of Two or more of the Provinces.

11. The Incorporation of Companies with Provincial Objects.

12. The Solemnization of Marriage in the Province.

13. Property and Civil Rights in the Province.

14. The Administration of Justice in the Province, including the Courts, both of Civil and of Criminal Jurisdiction, and including Procedure in Civil Matters in those Courts.

15. The Imposition of Punishment by Fine, Penalty, or Imprisonment for enforcing any Law of the Province made in relation to any Matter coming within any of the Classes of Subject enumerated in this Section.

16. Generally all Matters of a merely local or private Nature in the Province.

Education

93. In and for each Province the Legislature may exclusively make Laws in relation to Education, subject and according to the following Provisions:

1. Nothing in any such Law shall prejudicially affect any Right or Privilege with respect to Denominational Schools which any Class of Persons have by Law in the Province at the Union:

2. All the Powers, Privileges, and Duties at the Union by Law conferred and imposed in Upper Canada on the Separate Schools and School Trustees of the Queen's Roman Catholic Subjects shall be and the same are hereby extended to the Dissentient Schools of the Queen's Protestant and Roman Catholic Subjects in Quebec:

3. Where in any Province a System of Separate or Dissentient Schools exists by Law at the Union or is thereafter established by the Legislature of the Province, an Appeal shall lie to the Governor General in Council from any Act or Decision of any Provincial Authority affecting any Right or Privilege of the Protestant or Roman Catholic Minority of the Queen's Subjects in relation to Education:

4. In case any such Provincial Law as from Time to Time seems to the Governor General in Council requisite for the due Execution of the Provisions of this Section is not made, or in case any Decision of the Governor General in Council on any Appeal under this Section is not duly executed by the proper Provincial Authority in that Behalf, then and in every such Case, and as far only as the Circumstances of each Case require, the Parliament of Canada may make remedial Laws for the due Execution of the Provisions of this Section and of any Decision of the Governor General in Council under this Section.

Uniformity of Laws in Ontario, Nova Scotia, and New Brunswick

94. Notwithstanding anything in this Act, the Parliament of Canada may make Provision for the Uniformity of all or any of the Laws relative to Property and Civil Rights in Ontario, Nova Scotia, and New Brunswick, and of the Procedure of all or any of the Courts in those Three Provinces, and from and after the passing of any Act in that Behaf the Power of the

Parliament of Canada to make Laws in relation to any Matter comprised in any such Act shall, notwithstanding anything in this Act, be unrestricted; but any Act of the Parliament of Canada making Provision for such Uniformity shall not have effect in any Province unless and until it is adopted and enacted as Law by the Legislature thereof.

Agriculture and Immigration

95. In each Province the Legislature may make Laws in relation to Agriculture in the Province, and to Immigration into the Province; and it is hereby declared that the Parliament of Canada may from Time to Time make Laws in relation to Agriculture in all or any of the Provinces, and to Immigration into all or any of the Provinces; and any Law of the Legislature of a Province relative to Agriculture or to Immigration shall have effect in and for the Province as long and as far only as it is not repugnant to any Act of the Parliament of Canada.

VII. JUDICATURE

96. The Governor General shall appoint the Judges of the Superior, District, and County Courts in each Province, except those of the Courts of Probate in Nova Scotia and New Brunswick.

97. Until the Laws relative to Property and Civil Rights in Ontario, Nova Scotia, and New Brunswick, and the Procedure of the Courts of those Provinces are made uniform, the Judges of the Courts of those Provinces appointed by the Governor General shall be selected from the respective Bars of those Provinces.

98. The Judges of the Courts of Quebec shall be selected from the Bar of that Province.

99. The Judges of the Superior Courts shall hold office during good Behaviour, but shall be removable by the Governor General on Address of the Senate and House of Commons.

100. The Salaries, Allowances, and Pensions of the Judges of the Superior, District, and County Courts (except the Courts of Probate in Nova Scotia and New Brunswick), and of the Admiralty Courts in Cases where the Judges thereof are for the Time being paid by Salary, shall be fixed and provided by the Parliament of Canada.

101. The Parliament of Canada may, notwithstanding anything in this Act, from Time to Time, provide for the Constitution, Maintenance, and Organization of a General Court of Appeal for Canada, and for the Establishment of any additional Courts for the better Administration of the Laws of Canada.

VII. REVENUES; DEBTS; ASSETS; TAXATION

102. All Duties and Revenues over which the respective Legislatures of Canada, Nova Scotia, and New Brunswick before and at the Union had and have Power of Appropriation, except such portions thereof as are by this Act reserved to the respective Legislatures of the Provinces, or are raised by them in accordance with the special Powers conferred on them

by this Act, shall form One Consolidated Revenue Fund, to be appropriated for the Public Service of Canada in the Manner and subject to the Charges in this Act provided.

103. The Consolidated Revenue Fund of Canada shall be permanently charged with the Costs, Charges, and Expenses incident to the Collection, Management, and Receipt thereof, and the same shall form the first Charge thereon, subject to be reviewed and audited in such Manner as shall be ordered by the Governor General in Council until the Parliament otherwise provides.

104. The annual Interest of the Public Debts of the several Provinces of Canada, Nova Scotia, and New Brunswick at the Union shall form the Second Charge on the Consolidated Revenue Fund of Canada.

105. Unless altered by the Parliament of Canada, the salary of the Governor General shall be Ten Thousand Pounds Sterling Money of the United Kingdom of Great Britain and Ireland, payable out of the Consolidated Revenue Fund of Canada, and the same shall form the Third Charge thereon.

106. Subject to the several Payments by this Act charged on the Consolidated Revenue Fund of Canada, the same shall be appropriated by the Parliament of Canada for the Public Service.

107. All Stocks, Cash, Bankers' Balances, and Securities for Money belonging to each Province at the time of the Union, except as in this Act mentioned, shall be the Property of Canada, and shall be taken in Reduction of the amount of the respective Debts of the Provinces at the Union.

108. The Public Works and Property of each Province, enumerated in the Third Schedule to this Act, shall be the property of Canada.

109. All Lands, Mines, Minerals, and Royalties belonging to the several Provinces of Canada, Nova Scotia, and New Brunswick at the Union, and all Sums then due or payable for such Lands, Mines, Minerals, or Royalties, shall belong to the several Provinces of Ontario, Quebec, Nova Scotia, and New Brunswick in which the same are situate or arise, subject to any Trusts existing in respect thereof, and to any Interest other than that of the Province in the same.

110. All Assets connected with such Portions of the Public Debt of each Province as are assumed by that Province shall belong to that Province.

111. Canada shall be liable for the Debts and Liabilities of each Province existing at the Union.

112. Ontario and Quebec conjointly shall be liable to Canada for the amount (if any) by which the Debt of the Province of Canada exceeds at the Union Sixty-two million five hundred thousand dollars, and shall be charged with Interest at the Rate of Five per Centum per Annum thereon.

113. The Assets enumerated in the Fourth Schedule to this Act belonging at the Union to the Province of Canada shall be the Property of Ontario and Quebec conjointly.

114. Nova Scotia shall be liable to Canada for the Amount (if any) by which its Public Debt exceeds at the Union Eight million Dollars, and shall be charged with Interest at the Rate of Five per Centum per Annum thereon.

115. New Brunswick shall be liable to Canada for the Amount (if any)

by which its Public Debt exceeds at the Union Seven million Dollars, and shall be charged with Interest at the Rate of Fiver per Centum per Annum thereon.

116. In case the Public Debts of Nova Scotia and New Brunswick do not at the Union amount to Eight million and Seven million Dollars respectively, they shall receive by half-yearly Payments in advance from the Government of Canada, interest at Five per Centum per Annum on the Difference between the actual Amounts of their respective Debts and such stipulated Amounts.

117. The several Provinces shall retain all their respective Public Property not otherwise disposed of in this Act, subject to the Right of Canada to assume any Lands or Public Property required for Fortifications or for the Defense of the Country.

118. The following Sums shall be paid yearly by Canada to the several Provinces for the Support of their Government and Legislature:

Ontario. . . . . .Eighty Thousand Dollars

Quebec. . . . . .Seventy Thousand Dollars

New Brunswick. . . . . .Fifty Thousand Dollars

Nova Scotia. . . . . .Sixty Thousand Dollars

Two hundred and Sixty Thousand Dollars; and an annual Grant in aid of each Province shall be made equal to Eighty Cents per Head of the Population as ascertained by the Census of One thousand eight hundred and sixty-one, and in the Case of Nova Scotia and New Brunswick, by each subsequent Decennial Census until the Population of each of those two Provinces amounts to Four hundred thousand Souls, at which Rate such Grant shall thereafter remain. Such Grants shall be in full Settlement of all future Demands on Canada, and shall be paid half-yearly in advance to each Province; but the Government of Canada shall deduct from such Grants, as against any Province, all Sums chargeable as Interest on the Public Debt of that Province in excess of the several Amounts stipulated in this Act.

119. New Brunswick shall receive by half-yearly Payments in advance from Canada for the Period of Ten years from the Union an additional Allowance of Sixty-three thousand dollars per Annum; but as long as the Public Debt of that Province remains under Seven million Dollars, a Deduction equal to the Interest at Five per Centum per Annum on such Deficiency shall be made from that Allowance of Sixty-three thousand Dollars.

120. All Payments to be made under this Act, or in discharge of Liabilities created under any Act of the Provinces of Canada, Nova Scotia, and New Brunswick respectively, and assumed by Canada, shall, until the Parliament of Canada otherwise directs, be made in such Form and Manner as may from Time to Time be ordered by the Governor General in Council.

121. All Articles of the Growth, Produce, or Manufacture of any one

of the Provinces shall, from and after the Union, be admitted free into each of the other Provinces.

122. The Customs and Excise Laws of each Province shall, subject to the Provisions of this Act, continue in force until altered by the Parliament of Canada.

123. Where Customs Duties are, at the Union, leviable on any Goods, Wares, or Merchandises in any Two Provinces, those Goods, Wares, and Merchandises may, from and after the Union, be imported from one of those Provinces into the other of them on Proof of Payment of the Customs Duty leviable thereon in the Province of Exportation, and on Payment of such further Amount (if any) of Customs Duty as is leviable thereon in the Province of Importation.

124. Nothing in this Act shall affect the Right of New Brunswick to levy the Lumber Dues provided in Chapter Fifteen on Title Three of the Revised Statutes of New Brunswick, or in any Act amending that Act before or after the Union, and not increasing the Amount of such Dues; but the Lumber of any of the Provinces other than New Brunswick shall not be subject to such Dues.

125. No Lands or Property belonging to Canada or any Province shall be liable to Taxation.

126. Such Portions of the Duties and Revenues over which the respective Legislatures of Canada, Nova Scotia, and New Brunswick had before the Union Power of Appropriation as are by this Act reserved to the respective Governments or Legislatures of the Provinces, and all Duties and Revenues raised by them in accordance with the special Powers conferred upon them by this Act, shall in each Province form One Consolidated Revenue Fund to be appropriated for the Public Service of the Province.

IX. MISCELLANEOUS PROVISIONS

General

127. If any Person being at the passing of this Act a Member of the Legislative Council of Canada, Nova Scotia, or New Brunswick, to whom a Place in the Senate is offered, does not within Thirty Days thereafter, by Writing under his Hand addressed to the Governor General of the Province of Canada or to the Lieutenant-Governor of Nova Scotia or New Brunswick (as the Case may be) accept the same, he shall be deemed to have declined the same; and any Person who, being at the passing of this Act a Member of the Legislative Council of Nova Scotia or New Brunswick, accepts a Place in the Senate shall thereby vacate his Seat in such Legislative Council.

128. Every Member of the Senate or House of Commons of Canada shall before taking his Seat therein take and subscribe before the Governor General or some Person authorized by him, and every Member of a Legislative Council or Legislative Assembly of any Province shall before taking his Seat therein take and subscribe before the Lieutenant Governor of the Province or some Person authorized by him, the Oath of Allegiance contained in the Fifth Schedule to this Act; and every Member of the Senate

of Canada and every Member of the Legislative Council of Quebec shall also, before taking his Seat therein, take and subscribe before the Governor General, or some Person authorized by him, the Declaration of Qualification contained in the same Schedule.

129. Except as otherwise provided by this Act, all Laws in force in Canada, Nova Scotia, or New Brunswick at the Union, and all Courts of Civil and Criminal Jurisdiction, and all legal Commissions, Powers, and Authorities, and all Officers, Judicial, Administrative, and Ministerial, existing therein at the Union, shall continue in Ontario, Quebec, Nova Scotia, and New Brunswick respectively, as if the Union had not been made; subject nevertheless (except with respect to such as are enacted by or exist under Acts of the Parliament of Great Britain or of the Parliament of the United Kingdom of Great Britain and Ireland) to be repealed, abolished, or altered by the Parliament of Canada, or by the Legislature of the respective Province, according to the Authority of the Parliament or of that Legislature under this Act.

130. Until the Parliament of Canada otherwise provides, all Officers of the several Provinces having Duties to discharge in relation to Matters other than those coming within the Classes of Subjects by this Act assigned exclusively to the Legislatures of the Provinces shall be Officers of Canada, and shall continue to discharge the Duties of their respective Offices under the same Liabilities, Responsibilities, and Penalties as if the Union had not been made.

131. Until the Parliament of Canada otherwise provides, the Governor General in Council may from Time to Time appoint such Officers as the Governor General in Council deems necessary or proper for the effectual Execution of this Act.

132. The Parliament and Government of Canada shall have all Powers necessary or proper for performing the Obligations of Canada or any Province thereof, as Part of the British Empire, towards Foreign Countries, arising under Treaties between the Empire and such Foreign Countries.

133. Either the English or the French Language may be used by any Person in the Debates of the Houses of the Parliament of Canada and of the Houses of the Legislature of Quebec; and both those Languages shall be used in the respective Records and Journals of those Houses; and either of those Languages may be used by any Person or in any Pleading or Process in or issuing from any Court of Canada established under this Act, and in or from all or any of the Courts of Quebec.

The Acts of the Parliament of Canada and of the Legislature of Quebec shall be printed and published in both those Languages.

Ontario and Quebec

134. Until the Legislature of Ontario or of Quebec otherwise provides, the Lieutenant-Governors of Ontario and Quebec may each appoint under the Great Seal of the Province the following Officers, to hold Office during Pleasure, that is to say, -- the Attorney-General, the Secretary and Registrar of the Province, the Treasurer of the Province, the Commissioner of Crown Lands, and the Commissioner of Agriculture and Public Works, and in the Case of Quebec the Soliciter General and may,

by Order of the Lieutenant-Governor in Council, from Time to Time prescribe the Duties of those Officers and of the several Departments over which they shall preside or to which they shall belong, and of the Officers and Clerks thereof; and may also appoint other and additional Officers to hold office during Pleasure, and may from Time to Time prescribe the Duties of those Officers, and of the several Departments over which they shall preside or to which they shall belong, and of the Officers and Clerks thereof.

135. Until the Legislature of Ontario or Quebec otherwise provides, all Rights, Powers, Duties, Functions, Responsibilities, or Authorities at the passing of this Act vested in or imposed on the Attorney-General, Soclicitor General, Secretary and Registrar of the Province of Canada, Minister of Finance, Commissioner of Crown Lands, Commissioner of Public Works, and Minister of Agriculture and Receiver General, by any Law, Statute or Ordinance of Upper Canada, Lower Canada, or Canada, and not repugnant to this Act, shall be vested in or imposed on any Officer to be appointed by the Lieutenant-Governor for the Discharge of the same or any of them; and the Commissioner of Agriculture and Public Works shall perform the Duties and Functions of the Office of Minister of Agriculture at the passing of this Act imposed by the Law of the Province of Canada, as well as those of the Commissioner of Public works.

136. Until altered by the Lieutenant-Governor in Council, the Great Seals of Ontario and Quebec repectively shall be the same, or of the same Design, as those used in the Provinces of Upper Canada and Lower Canada respectively before their Union as the Province of Canada.

137. The Words "and from thence to the End of the then next ensuing Session of the Legislature" or Words to the same Effect, used in any temporary Act of the Province of Canada not expired before the Union, shall be construed to extend and apply to the next Session of the Parliament of Canada if the subject matter of the Act is within the Powers of the same, as defined by this Act, or to the next Session of the Legislatures of Ontario and Quebec respectively if the subject matter of the Act is within the Powers of the same as defined by this Act.

138. From and after the Union the Use of the Words "Upper Canada" instead of "Ontario", or "Lower Canada" instead of "Quebec" in any Deed, Writ, Process, Pleading, Document, Matter or Thing, shall not invalidate the same.

139. Any Proclamation under the Great Seal of the Province of Canada issued before the Union to take effect at a Time which is subsequent to the Union, whether relating to that Province, or to Upper Canada, or to Lower Canada, and the several Matters and Things therein proclaimed shall be and continue of like Force and Effect as if the Union had not been made.

140. Any Proclamation which is authorized by any Act of the Legislature of the Province of Canada to be issued under the Great Seal of the Province of Canada, whether relating to that Province, or to Upper Canada, or to Lower Canada, and which is not issued before the Union, may be issued by the Lieutenant-Governor of Ontario or of Quebec, as its Subject Matter requires, under the Great Seal thereof; and from and after the Issue of such Proclamation the same and the several Matters and Things therein proclaimed shall be and continue of the like Force and Effect in

Ontario or Quebec as if the Union had not been made.

141. The Penitentiary of the Province of Canada shall, until the Parliament of Canada otherwise provides, be and continue the Penitentiary of Ontario and of Quebec.

142. The Division and Adjustment of the Debts, Credits, Liabilities, Properties, and Assets of Upper Canada and Lower Canada shall be referred to the Arbitrament of Three Arbitrators, One chosen by the Government of Ontario, One by the Government of Quebec, and One by the Government of Canada; and the Selection of Arbitrators shall not be made until the Parliament of Canada and the Legislatures of Ontario and Quebec have met; and the Arbitrator chosen by the Government of Canada shall not be a Resident either in Ontario or in Quebec.

143. The Governor General in Council may from Time to Time order that such and so many of the Records, Books, and Documents of the Province of Canada as he thinks fit shall be appropriated and delivered either to Ontario or to Quebec and the same shall thenceforth be the Property of that Province; and any Copy thereof or Extract therefrom, duly cerified by the Officer having charge of the Original thereof, shall be admitted as Evidence.

144. The Lieutenant-Governor of Quebec may from Time to Time, by proclamation under the Great Seal of the Province, to take effect from a day to be appointed therein, constitute Townships in those Parts of the Province of Quebec in which Townships are not then already constituted, and fix the Metes and Bounds thereof.

X. INTERCOLONIAL RAILWAY

145. Inasmuch as the Provinces of Canada, Nova Scotia, and New Brunswick have joined in a Declaration that the Construction of the Intercolonial Railway is essential to the Consolidation of the Union of British North America, and to the Assent thereto of Nova Scotia and New Brunswick, and have consequently agreed that Provision should be made for its immediate Construction by the Government of Canada: Therefore, in order to give effect to that Agreement, it shall be the Duty of the Government and Parliament of Canada to provide for the Commencement within Six Months after the Union, of a Railway connecting the River St. Lawrence with the City of Halifax in Nova Scotia, and for the Construction thereof without Intermission, and the Completion thereof with all practicable Speed.

XI. ADMISSION OF OTHER COLONIES

146. It shall be lawful for the Queen, by and with the Advice of Her Majesty's Most Honourable Privy Council, on Addresses from the Houses of the Parliament of Canads, and from the Houses of the respective Legislatures of the Colonies or Provinces of Newfoundland, Prince Edward Island, and British Columbia, to admit those Colonies or Provinces, or any of them, into the Union, and on Address from the Houses of the Parliament of Canada to admit Rupert's Land and the North-western Territory, or either of them, into the Union, on such Terms and Conditions in each Case as are in the Addresses expressed and as the Queen thinks fit to

approve, subject to the Provisions of this Act; and the Provisions of any Order in Council in that Behalf shall have effect as if they had been enacted by the Parliament of the United Kingdom of Great Britain and Ireland.

147. In case of the Admission of Newfoundland and Prince Edward Island, or either of them, each shall be entitled to a Representation in the Senate of Canada of Four Members, and (notwithstanding anything in this Act) in case of the Admission of Newfoundland the normal Number of senators shall be Seventy-six and their maximun Number shall be Eighty-two but Prince Edward Island when admitted shall be deemed to be comprised in the third of the Three Divisions into which Canada is, in relation to the Constitution of the Senate, divided by this Act, and accordingly, after the Admission of Prince Edward Island, whether Newfoundland is admitted or not, the Representation of Nova Scotia and New Brunswick in the Senate shall, as Vacancies occur, be reduced from Twelve to Ten Members respectively, and the Representation of each of those Provinces shall not be increased at any Time beyond Ten, except under the Provision of this Act for the Appointment of Three or Six additional Senators under the Direction of the Queen.

THE STATUTE OF WESTMINSTER

Introduction

The Statutes of Westminster, 1931, arose out of the declarations of two Imperial Conferences held in 1926 and 1930. The Dominions participating at these two conferences were Canada, Australia, New Zealand, South Africa, the Irish Free State, Newfoundland (at that time still independent from Canada), and India (not affected by the Statute). The Act grants practicable political autonomy to the Dominions and provided for the repeal of several important colonial Acts. Among these were the Colonial Laws Validity Act of 1865, part of the Merchant Shipping Act of 1894, and part of the Colonial Courts of Admiralty Act of 1890 in so far as they interfered with the law-making functions of the Dominions. Their new status within the British Commonwealth is best described in a passage often quoted from the report of the Inter-Imperial Relations Committee of the Imperial Conference of 1926 usually called "The Balfour Declaration":

> They are autonomous communities within the British Empire, equal in status, in no way subordinate one to another in any aspect of their domestic or external affairs, though united by a common allegiance to the Crown, and freely associated as members of the British Commonwealth. (Imperial Conference, 1926, Summary of Proceedings, p. 12)

This Act was of extreme constitutional importance to Canada as it granted the right for the Canadian people to shape their own future and make their own policies at home and abroad.

STATUTE OF WESTMINSTER, 1931

22 GEORGE V, CHAPTER 4

A. D. 1931   ARRANGEMENT OF SECTIONS

STATUTE OF WESTMISTER, 1931
22 GEORGE V, CHAPTER 4

An Act to give effect to certain resolutions passed by Imperial Conference held in the years 1926 and 1930

11th December, 1931.

Whereas the delegates to His Majesty's Governments in the United Kingdom, the Dominion of Canada, the Commonwealth of Australia, the Dominion of New Zealand, the Union of South Africa, the Irish Free State and Newfoundland, at Imperial Conferences holden at Westminster in the years of our Lord nineteen hundred and twenty-six and nineteen hundred and thirty did concur in making the declarations and resolutions set forth in the Reports of the said Conferences:

And whereas it is meet and proper to set out by way of preamble to this Act that, inasmuch as the Crown is the symbol of the free association of the members of the British Commonwealth of Nations, and as they are united by a common allegiance to the Crown, it would be in accord with the established constitutional position of all the members of the Commonwealth in relation to one another that any alteration in the law touching the

Succession to the Throne or the Royal Style and Titles shall hereafter require the assent as well of the Parliaments of all the Dominions as of the Parliament of the United Kingdom:

And whereas it is in accord with the established constitutional position that no law hereafter made by the Parliament of the United Kingdom shall extend to any of the said Dominions as part of the law of that Dominion otherwise than at the request and with the consent of that Dominion.

And whereas it is necessary for the ratifying, confirming and establishing of certain of the said declarations and resolutions of the said Conferences that a law be made and enacted in due form by authority of the Parliament of the United Kingdom:

And whereas the Dominion of Canada, the Commonwealth of Australia, the Dominion of New Zealand, the Union of South Africa, the Irish Free State and Newfoundland have severally requested and consented to the submission of a measure to the Parliament of the United Kingdom for making such provision with regard to the matters aforesaid as is hereafter in this Act contained:

Now, therefore, be in enacted by the King's Most Excellent Majesty by and with the advice and consent of the Lords Spiritual and Temporal, and Commons, in this present Parliament assembled, and by the authority of the same, as follows:

1. In this Act the expression "Dominion" means any of the following Dominions, that is to say, the Dominion of Canada, the Commonwealth of Australia, the Dominion of New Zealand, the Union of South Africa, the Irish Free State and Newfoundland.

2. (1) The Colonial Laws Validity Act, 1865, shall not apply to any law made after the commencement of this Act by the Parliament of a Dominion.

(2) No law and no provision of any law made after the commencement of this Act by the Parliament of a Dominion shall be void or inoperative on the ground that it is repugnant to the law of England, or to the provisions of any existing or future Act of Parliament of the United Kingdom, or to any order, rule, or regulation made under any such Act, and the powers of the Parliament of a Dominion shall include the power to repeal or amend any such Act, order, rule or regulation in so far as the same is part of the law of the Dominion.

3. It is hereby declared and enacted that the Parliament of a Dominion has full power to make laws having extra-territorial operation.

4. No Act of Parliament of the United Kingdom passed after the commencement of this Act shall extend or be deemed to extend, to a Dominion as part of the law of that Dominion, unless it is expressly declared in that Act that that Dominion has requested, and consented to, the enactment thereof.

5. Without prejudice to the generality of the foregoing provisions of this Act, sections seven hundred and thirty-five and seven hundred and thirty-six of the Merchant Shipping Act, 1894, shall be construed as though reference therein to the Legislature of a British possession did not include

reference to the Parliament of a Dominion.

6. Without prejudice to a generality of the foregoing provisions of this Act, section four of the Colonial Courts of Admiralty Act, 1890 (which requires certain laws to be reserved for the signification of His Majesty's pleasure or to contain a suspending clause), and so much of section seven of that Act as requires the approval of His Majesty in Council to any rules of Court for regulating the practice and procedure of a Colonial Court of Admiralty, shall cease to have effect in any Dominion as from the commencement of this Act.

7. (1) Nothing in this Act shall be deemed to apply to the repeal, amendment or alteration of the British North America Acts, 1867 to 1930, or any order, rule or regulation made thereunder.

(2) The provisions of section two of this Act shall extend to laws made by any of the Provinces of Canada and to the powers of the legislatures of such Provinces.

(3) The powers conferred by this Act upon the Parliament of Canada or upon the legislatures of the Provinces shall be restricted to the enactment of laws in relation to matters within the competence of the Parliament of Canada or of any of the legislatures of the Provinces respectively.

8. Nothing in this Act shall be deemed to confer any power to repeal or alter the Constitution or the Constitution Act of the Commonwealth of Australia or the Constitution Act of the Dominion of New Zealand otherwise than in accordance with the law existing before the commencement of this Act.

9. (1) Nothing in this Act shall be deemed to authorize the Parliament of the Commonwealth of Australia to make laws on any matter within the authority of the States of Australia, not being a matter within the authority of the Parliament or Government of the Commonwealth of Australia.

(2) Nothing in this Act shall be deemed to require the concurrence of the Parliament or Government of the Commonwealth of Australia, in any law made by the Parliament of the United Kingdom with respect to any matter within the authority of the States of Australia, not being a matter within the authority of the Parliament or Government of the Commonwealth of Australia, in any case where it would have been in accordance with the constitutional practice existing before the commencement of this Act that the Parliament of the United Kingdom shoud make that law without such concurrence.

(3) In the application of this Act to the Commonwealth of Australia the request and consent referred to in section four shall mean the request and consent of the Parliament and Government of the Commonwealth.

10. (1) None of the following sections of this Act, that is to say, sections two, three, four, five and six, shall extend to a Dominion to which this section applies as part of the law of that Dominion unless that section is adopted by the Parliament of the Dominion, and any Act of that Parliament adopting any section of this Act may provide that the adoption shall have effect either from the commencement of this Act or from such later

date as is specified in the adopting Act.

(2) The Parliament of any such Dominion as aforesaid may at any time revoke the adoption of any section referred to in subsection (1) of this section.

(3) The Dominions to which this section applies are the Commonwealth of Australia, the Dominion of New Zealand and Newfoundland.

11. Notwithstanding anything in the Interpretation Act, 1889, the expression "Colony" shall not, in any Act of the Parliament of the United Kingdom passed after the commencement of this Act, include a Dominion or any Province or State forming part of a Dominion.

12. This Act may be cited as the Statute of Westminster, 1931.

AREA AND POPULATION OF CANADA AND THE PROVINCES

Province	Population June 1972	Land Area Sq. Miles
Newfoundland	526,500	143,045
Prince Edward Island	112,500	2,184
Nova Scotia	802,400	20,402
New Brunswick	639,900	27,835
Quebec	6,114,100	523,860
Ontario	7,814,900	344,092
Manitoba	996,700	211,755
Saskatchewan	934,200	220,182
Alberta	1,649,200	248,800
British Columbia	2,216,200	359,279
Territories	55,300	1,458,784
Canada	21,861,900	3,560,238

POPULATION OF MAJOR METROPOLITAN AREAS, JUNE 1971 CENSUS

Montreal	2,743,208
Toronto	2,268,043
Vancouver	1,082,352
Ottawa-Hull	602,510
Winnipeg	540,362
Hamilton	498,523
Edmonton	495,702
Quebec	480,502
Calgary	403,319
Niagara-St. Catharines	303,429
London	286,011
Windsor	258,643
Kitchener	226,846
Halifax	222,637
Victoria	195,800
Sudbury	155,424
Regina	140,734

The following items are by no means intended to constitute
a bibliography of Canadian history, but rather represent
a random survey of works on different aspects of Canadian
history. Many of the items listed have their own bibliographies which will give further readings in any specific
area.

SERIES

Canada and Its Provinces: A History of the Canadian People and Their
Institutions, by One Hundred Associates. 23 vols. Ed. Adam Shortt and
Arthur G. Doughty.   Toronto: Brook, 1917.

Canadian Historical Booklets Series. Ottawa: Canadian Historical Association.

Canadian Historical Documents Series. Ottawa: Canadian Historical Association.

Champlain Society Publications.   Toronto: Champlain Society.

Hudson's Bay Record Society Publications. 25 vols. London: Hudson's
Bay Record Society, 1948-63.

The Makers of Canada: University Edition. 11 vols. Toronto: Morang,
1912.

GENERAL

Audet, Francis J.   Canadian Historical Dates and Events.   Ottawa: George
Beauregard, 1917.

Brebner, John Bartlet. North Atlantic Triangle. New York: Columbia
University Press, 1958.

Brown, George William, ed.   Canada.   Berkeley: University of California
Press, 1950.

Burpee, Lawrence Johnstone, ed.   An Historical Atlas of Canada.   Toronto:
Nelson, 1927.

Burt, Alfred Leroy.   The United States, Great Britain & British North
America. . . .   New York: Russell & Russell, 1961.

Careless, J. M. S.   Canada: A Story of Challenge.   3rd ed.   Toronto:
Macmillan, 1970.

Careless, J. M. S., ed.   The Canadians, 1867-1967.   New York: St. Martin's
Press, 1967.

Clark, Samuel Delbert. The Social Development of Canada: An Intro-
ductory Study with Select Documents. Toronto: University of Toronto
Press, 1942.

Cook, George Ramsay, et al.   Canada: A Modern Study.   Toronto: Clarke,
Irwin, 1963.

Creighton, Donald Grant.   Dominion of the North: A History of Canada.
Toronto: Macmillan, 1957.

Flenley, Ralph, ed.   Essays in Canadian History.   Toronto: Macmillan,
1939.

Lower, J. A.   Canada: An Outline History.   Toronto: Ryerson Press, 1966.

Lower, Arthur Reginald Marsden.   Canadians in the Making: A Social
History of Canada.   Toronto: Longmans, Green, 1958.

Lower, Arthur Reginald Marsden.   Colony to Nation: A History of Canada.
Toronto: Longmans, Green, 1958.

McInnis, Edgar Wardwell.   Canada: A Political and Social History.   Rev.
and enl.   New York: Holt, Rinehart, 1959.

Martin, Chester Bailey.   Foundations of Canadian Nationhood.   Toronto:
University of Toronto Press, 1955.

Morton, William Lewis.   The Canadian Identity.   Madison: University of
Wisconsin Press, 1961.

Morton, W. L.   The Critical Years: The Union of British North America,
1857-1873.   Toronto: McClelland and Stewart, 1964.

Parkman, Francis.   Works.   Frontnac Edition.   Boston: Little, Brown,
1901-10.

Porter, John A.   The Vertical Mosaic: An Analysis of Social Class and
Power in Canada.   Toronto: University of Toronto Press, 1965.

Taplin, Glen W.   Canadian Chronology.   Metuchen, N. J.: Scarecrow
Press, 1970.

REGIONAL

Alvord, Clarence Walworth.   The Mississippi Valley in British Politics.
New York: Russell & Russell, 1959.

Angus, Henry Forbes, ed.   British Columbia and the United States.
Toronto: Ryerson Press, 1942.

Berton, Pierre.   The Klondike Fever: The Life and Death of the Last Great
Gold Rush.   New York: Knopf, 1959.

Brebner, John Bartlet. The Neutral Yankees of Nova Scotia. New York: Columbia University Press, 1937.

Craig, Gerald Marquis, ed. Early Travellers in the Canadas, 1791-1867. Toronto: Macmillan, 1955.

Cruikshank, Ernest Alexander. The Settlement of the United Empire Loyalists on the Upper St. Lawrence and Bay of Quinte in 1784: A Documentary Record. . . . Toronto: Ontario Historical Society, 1934.

Eccles, W. J. Canada Under Louis XIV, 1663-1701. Toronto: McClelland & Stewart, 1964.

England, Robert. The Colonization of Western Canada: A Study of Contemporary Land Settlement, 1896-1934. London: P. S. King, 1936.

Fuller, George Washington. A History of the Pacific Northwest. New York: Knopf, 1958.

Hedges, James Blaine. Building the Canadian West: The Land and Colonization Policies of the Canadian Pacific Railway. New York: Macmillan, 1939.

Howard, Joseph Kinsey. Strange Empire: A Narrative of the Northwest. New York: Morrow, 1952.

Howay, Frederick William. British Columbia: The Making of a Province. Toronto: Ryerson Pess, 1928.

Lent, D. Geneva. West of the Mountains: James Sinclair and the Hudson's Bay Company. Seattle: University of Washington Press, 1963.

MacEwan, John Walter Grant. Between the Red and the Rockies. Toronto: University of Toronto Press, 1953.

MacKay, Robert Alexander, ed. Newfoundland: Economic, Diplomatic and Strategic Studies. Toronto: Oxford University Press, 1946.

MacLeod, Margaret Arnett, and W. L. Norton. Cuthbert Grant of Grantown: Warden of the Plains of Red River. Toronto: McClelland & Stewart, 1963.

MacNutt, W. S. The Atlantic Provinces: The Emergence of Colonial Society, 1712-1857. Toronto: McClelland & Stewart, 1965.

MacNutt, William Stewart. New Brunswick: A History, 1784-1867. Toronto: Macmillan, 1963.

MacPherson, Crawford Brough. Democracy in Alberta. Toronto: University of Toronto Press, 1953.

Morton, Arthur Silver. History of Prairie Settlement. Toronto: Macmillan, 1935.

Morton, William Lewis. Manitoba: A History. Toronto: University of Toronto Press, 1957.

Ormsby, Margaret Anchoretta. British Columbia: A History. Vancouver: B. C.: Macmillan, 1958.

Parsons, John E. West on the 49th Parallel: Red River to the Rockies, 1877-1876. New York: William Morrow, 1963.

Patterson, George. Studies in Nova Scotian History. Halifax, N. S.: Imperial, 1940.

Pritchett, John Perry. The Red River Valley, 1811-1849: A Regional Study. New Haven, Conn.: Yale University Press, 1942.

Neatby, Hilda Marion. Quebec: The Revolutionary Age, 1760-1791. Toronto: McClelland & Stewart, 1966.

Stanley, George Francis Gilman. The Birth of Western Canada: A History of the Riel Rebellions. London: Longmans, Green, 1936.

Whitelaw, William Menzies. The Maritime and Canada before Confederation. Toronto: Oxford University Press, 1934.

NEW FRANCE AND FRENCH CANADA

Burt, Alfred Leroy. The Old Province of Quebec. Toronto: Ryerson Press, 1933.

Caldwell, Norman Ward. The French in the Mississippi Valley, 1740-1750. Urbana, Ill.: University of Illinois Press, 1941.

Champlain, Samuel de. The Voyages and Explorations, 1604-1616. New York: Allerton, 1922.

Cole, Charles Woolsey. Colbert and a Century of French Mercantilism. New York: Columbia University Press, 1939.

Desbarats, Peter. The State of Quebec: A Journalist's View of the Quiet Revolution. Toronto: McClelland & Stewart, 1964.

Falardeau, Jean Charles, ed. Essays on Contemporary Quebec. Quebec: Laval University Press, 1953.

Hughes, Everett Cherrington. French Canada in Transition. Chicago: University of Chicago Press, 1943.

Lanctot, Gustave. Histoire du Canada: II: Du Regime Royal au Trait d' Utrecht, 1663-1713. English edition. Montreal: Lib. Beauchemin, 1963.

Lanctot, Gustave. A History of Canada. Trans. Josephine Hambleton. Cambridge, Mass.: Harvard University Press, 1963.

Manning, Helen. The Revolt of French Canada, 1800-1835. Toronto: Macmillan, 1962.

Pierre Jérôme, Brother. The Impertinences of Brother Anonymous. Pref. André Laurendeau. Trans. Miriam Chapin. Montreal: Harvest House, 1962.

Rioux, Marcel. French Canadian Society. Toronto: McClelland & Stewart, 1964.

Scott, Francis Reginald, ed. Quebec States Her Case: Speeches and Articles from Quebec in the Years of Unrest. Toronto: Macmillan, 1964.

Siegfried, André. The Race Question in Canada. Ed. Frank H. Underhill. Toronto: McClelland & Stewart, 1966.

Sloan, Thomas. Quebec: The Not So Quiet Revolution. Toronto: Ryerson Press, 1965.

Wade, Mason. The French-Canadian Outlook: A Brief Account of the Unknown North Americans. New York: Viking Press, 1946.

Wade, Mason. The French Canadians, 1760-1945. London: Macmillan, 1955.

Wrong, George Mackinnon. The Rise and Fall of New France. Toronto: Macmillan, 1928.

EXPLORATION

Brebner, John Bartlet. Explorers of North America, 1492-1806. Garden City, N. Y.: Doubleday, 1955.

Burpee, Lawrence Johnstone. The Discovery of Canada. Toronto: Macmillan, 1946.

Burpee, Lawrence Johnstone. The Search for the Western Sea. 2 vols. Toronto: Macmillan, 1935.

Dodge, Ernest Stanley. Northwest by Sea. . . . New York: Oxford University Press, 1961.

Downey, Fairfax Davis. Louisbourg: Key to a Continent. Englewood Cliffs, N. J.: Prentice-Hall, 1963.

Mackenzie, Alexander. Voyages from Montreal through the Continent of North America to the Frozen and Pacific Oceans. . . . New York: Allerton Books, 1922.

Neatby, Leslie Hamilton. The Quest of the Northwest Passage. London: Constable, 1959.

Nute, Grace Lee. Caesars of the Wilderness: Médard Chouart, Sieur des Groseilliers and Pierre Esprit Radisson, 1618-1710. New York: Appleton-Century, 1943.

Oleson, Trygvi J. Early Voyages and Northern Approaches, 1000-1632. Toronto: McClelland & Stewart, 1964.

Vail, Philip. The Magnificent Adventures of Alexander Mackenzie. New York: Dodd, Mead, 1964.

Vestal, Stanley. King of the Fur Traders. Boston: Houghton Mifflin, 1940.

Warkentin, John. The Western Interior of Canada: A Recount of Geographical Discovery 1612-1917. Toronto: McClelland & Stewart, 1964.

ECONOMICS (INCL. FUR TRADE)

Campbell, Marjorie Elliott. McGillivray: Lord of the Northwest. Toronto: Clarke, Irwin, 1962.

Campbell, Marjorie Elliot. The North West Company. Toronto: Macmillan, 1957.

Camu, Pierre, et al. Economic Geography of Canada. Toronto: Macmillan, 1964.

Canada. Royal Commission on Banking and Currency in Canada. Report. Ottawa: King's Printer, 1933.

Canada. Royal Commission to Inquire into Railways and Transportation in Canada. Report. Ottawa: King's Printer, 1932.

Canada. Royal Grain Inquiry Commission. Report. Ottawa: King's Printer, 1925.

Currie, Archibald William. The Grand Trunk Railway of Canada. Toronto: University of Toronto Press, 1957.

Denison, Merrill. The Barley and the Stream: The Molson Story: A Footnote to Canadian History. Toronto: McClelland & Stewart, 1955.

Easterbrook, William Thomas, and Hugh G. Aitken. Canadian Economic History. Toronto: Macmillan, 1956.

Ellis, Lewis Ethan. Reciprocity 1911: A Study in Canadian-American Relations. New Haven, Conn.: Yale University Press, 1939.

Galbraith, John Semple. The Hudson's Bay Company as an Imperial Factor, 1821-1869. Toronto: University of Toronto Press, 1957.

Glazebrook, George Parkin. A History of Transportation in Canada. Toronto: Ryerson Press, 1938.

Innis, Harold Adams. Essays in Canadian Economic History. Toronto: University of Toronto Press, 1956.

Innis, Harold Adams. The Fur Trade in Canada. Toronto: University of Toronto Press, 1956.

Innis, Harold Adams. A History of the Canadian Pacific Railway. Toronto: McClelland & Stewart, 1932.

Innis, Harold Adams, ed. Select Documents in Canadian Economic History. 2 vols. Toronto: University of Toronto Press, 1929-33.

Lawson, Murray G. Fur: A Study in English Mercantilism, 1700-1755. Toronto: University of Toronto Press, 1943.

Logan, Harold Amos. State Intervention and Assistance in Collective Bargaining: The Canadian Experience, 1943-1954. Toronto: University of Toronto Press, 1956.

McGibbon, Duncan Alexander. The Canadian Grain Trade, 1931-1951. Toronto: University of Toronto Press, 1952.

McIvor, Russell Craig. Canadian Monetary, Banking, and Fiscal Development. Toronto: Macmillan, 1958.

MacKay, Douglas. The Honourable Company: A History of the Hudson's Company. 2nd ed. Toronto: McClelland & Stewart, 1949.

Tucker, Gilbert Norman. The Canadian Commercial Revolution, 1845-1851. New Haven, Conn.: Yale University Press, 1936.

Wallace, William Stewart. The Pedlars from Quebec. Toronto: Ryerson Press, 1954.

Wood, Louis Aubrey. A History of Farmers' Movements in Canada. Toronto: Ryerson Press, 1924.

POLITICS

Beck, James Murray. The Government of Nova Scotia. Toronto: University of Toronto Press, 1957.

Cornell, Paul Grant. The Alignment of Political Groups in Canada, 1841-1867. Toronto: University of Toronto Press, 1962.

Dafoe, John Wesley. Laurier: A Study in Canadian Politics. Toronto: Allen, 1922.

Dafoe, John Wesley. The Voice of Dafoe. Ed. W. L. Morton. Toronto: Macmillan, 1945.

Eggleston, Wilfred. The Road to Nationhood. Toronto: Oxford University Press, 1946.

Kerr, Donald Gordon Grady. Sir Edmund Head: A Scholarly Governor. Toronto: University of Toronto Press, 1954.

Lipset, Seymour Martin. Agrarian Socialism: The Cooperative Commonwealth Federation in Saskatchewan. Berkeley: University of California Press, 1959.

McNaught, Kenneth Williams Kirkpatrick. A Prophet in Politics: A Biography of J. S. Woodsworth. Toronto: University of Toronto Press, 1959.

Meighen, Arthur. Unrevised and Unrepented: Debating Speeches and Others. Toronto: Clarke, Irwin, 1949.

Quinn, Herbert Furlong. The Union Nationale: A Study in Quebec Nationalism. Toronto: University of Toronto Press, 1963.

Underhill, Frank Hawkins. In Search of Canadian Liberalism. Toronto: Macmillan, 1961.

Williams, John Ryan. The Conservative Party of Canada, 1920-1949. Durham, N. C.: Duke University Press, 1956.

CANADIAN CONSTITUTION

Bolger, Francis W. P. Prince Edward Island and Confederation: 1873-1963. Charlottetown, P. E. I.: St. Dunstan's University Press, 1964.

Canada, Public Archives. Documents Relating to the Constitutional History of Canada. Ottawa, King's Printer, 1935.

Clokie, Hugh Macdowall. Canadian Government and Politics. Rev. ed. Toronto: Longmans, 1950.

Cole, Taylor. The Canadian Bureaucracy. Durham, N. C.: Duke University Press, 1949.

Canada, Parliament. Confederation Debates in the Province of Canada. Toronto: McClelland & Stewart, 1963.

Coupland, Reginald. The Quebec Act: A Study in Statesmanship. Oxford: Clarendon Press, 1925.

Creighton, Donald Grant. The Road to Confederation. Toronto: Macmillan, 1964.

Dawson, Robert MacGregor. Constitutional Issues in Canada, 1900-1931. London: Oxford University Press, 1937.

Dawson, William Foster. Procedure in the Canadian House of Commons. Canadian Government Series 12. Toronto: University of Toronto Press, 1963.

Doughty, Arthur George, ed. The Elgin-Grey Papers, 1846-1952. Ottawa: Public Archives, 1937.

Dunham, Aileen. Political Unrest in Upper Canada, 1815-1836. Toronto: McClelland & Stewart, 1963.

Durham, John George Lambton, 1st Earl of. The Durham Report: An Abridged Version. Ed. Sir Reginald Coupland. Oxford: Clarendon Press, 1945.

Durham, John George Lambton. Report on the Affairs of British North America. Oxford: Clarendon Press, 1912.

Elgin, James B. Letters and Journals of James, Eighth Earl of Elgin. . . . London: J. Murray, 1872.

Gerin-Lajoie, Paul. Constitutional Amendment in Canada. Toronto: University of Toronto Press, 1950.

Gillis, Duncan Hugh. Democracy in the Canadas, 1759-1867. Toronto: Oxford University Press, 1951.

Kennedy, William Paul McClure. The Constitution of Canada, 1534-1937. 2nd ed. London: Oxford University Press, 1938.

Kennedy, W. P. M. Statutes, Treaties and Documents of the Canadian Constitution, 1713-1929. London, 1930.

McGee, Thomas D'Arcy. 1825-1925: A Collection of Speeches and Addresses. Toronto: Macmillan, 1937.

Mackay, Robert Alexander. The Unreformed Senate of Canada. Rev. ed. Toronto: McClelland & Stewart, 1963.

Mansergh, Nicholas. The Name and Nature of the British Commonwealth. Cambridge: Cambridge University Press, 1954.

Ollivier, Maurice. British North America Acts and Selected Statutes, 1867-1962. Ottawa: Queen's Printer, 1962.

Ollivier, Maurice. Problems of Canadian Sovereignty. Toronto: Canada Law Book, 1945.

Thomas, Lewis Herbert. The Struggle for Responsible Government in the Northwest Territories, 1807-1897. Toronto: University of Toronto Press, 1956.

Underhill, Frank Hawkins. The Image of Confederation, Toronto: Canadian Broadcasting Corporation, 1964.

Waite, Peter Busby. The Life and Times of Confederation, 1864-1867: Politics, Newspapers and the Union of British North America. Toronto: University of Toronto Press, 1962.

EXTERNAL AFFAIRS

Angus, Henry Forbes. Canada and the Far East, 1940-1953. Toronto: University of Toronto Press, 1953.

Brebner, John Bartlet. North Atlantic Triangle. New Haven, Conn.: Yale University Press, 1945.

Brown, Robert Craig. Canada's National Policy, 1883-1900: A Study in Canadian-American Relations. Princeton, N. J.: Princeton University Press, 1945.

Corbett, Percy Ellwood. The Settlement of the Canadian-American Disputes, Toronto: Ryerson Press, 1937.

Eayrs, James. The Art of the Possible. Toronto: University of Toronto Press, 1961.

Glazebrook, George Parkin de Twenebrokes. A History of Canadian External Relations, Toronto: Oxford University Press, 1950.

Gordon, J. King, ed. Canada's Role as a Middle Power: Papers Given at the Third Annual Banff Conference on World Development, August 1965. Toronto: Canadian Institute of International Affairs, 1966.

McInnis, Edgar. The Atlantic Triangle and the Cold War. Toronto: University of Toronto Press, 1959.

Mansergh, Nicholas. Problems of External Policy, 1931-1939. London: Oxford University Press, 1952.

Masters, Donald Campbell. The Reciprocity Treaty of 1854. Toronto: McClelland & Stewart, 1963.

Minifie, James MacDonald. Peacemaker or Powder Monkey: Canada's Role in a Revolutionary World. Toronto: McClelland & Stewart, 1960.

Pope, Maurice. Public Servant: The Memoirs of Sir Joseph Pope. Toronto, Oxford University Press, 1960.

Savelle, Max. The Diplomatic History of the Canadian Boundary, 1749-1763. New Haven, Conn.: Yale University Press, 1940.

Shippee, Lester Burrell. Canadian-American Relations, 1849-1874. . . . New Haven, Conn.: Yale University Press, 1939.

Smith, Goldwin Albert. The Treaty of Washington, 1871. Ithaca, N.Y.: Cornell University Press, 1941.

Tansill, Charles Callan. Canadian-American Relations 1875-1911. Toronto: Ryerson Press, 1943.

MILITARY

Anbury, Thomas. With Burgoyne from Quebec: An Account of the Life at Quebec and of the Famous Battle at Saratoga. Ed. Sydney W. Jackman. Toronto: Macmillan, 1963.

Bird, Harrison. Navies in the Mountains: The Battles on the Waters of Lake Champlain and Lake George 1609-1814. Toronto: Oxford University Press, 1962.

Brewin, Andrew. Stand on Guard: The Search for a Canadian Defense Policy. Toronto: Macmillan & Stewart, 1965.

Coupland, Reginald. American Revolution and British Empire. New York: Russell & Russell, 1965.

Dawson, Robert MacGregor. The Conscription Crisis of 1944. Toronto: University of Toronto Press, 1961.

Duguid, Archer Fortescue. Official History of the Canadian Forces in the Great War, 1914-1919. Ottawa: King's Printer, 1938.

Eayrs, James George. In Defence of Canada. 2 vols. Toronto: University of Toronto Press, 1965.

Hibbert, Christopher. Wolfe at Quebec. Toronto: Longmans, 1959.

Hitsman, J. Mackay. The Incredible War of 1812. Toronto: University of Toronto Press, 1965.

Nicholson, Gerald Wiiliam Lingen. The Canadian Expeditionary Force, 1914-1919. Ottawa: Queen's Printer, 1962.

Perkins, Bradford, ed. The Causes of the War of 1812. New York:
Holt, Rinehart, 1962.

Pope, Lt.-Gen. Maurice Arthur. Soldiers and Politicians: Memoirs.
Toronto: University of Toronto Press, 1962.

Samuel, Sigmund. The Seven Years War in Canada, 1756-1763. Toronto:
Ryerson Press, 1934.

Schull, John Joseph. The Far Distant Ships. Ottawa: Queen's Printer,
1961.

Simcoe, John Graves. Military Journal. Toronto: Baxter, 1962.

Stacey, Charles Perry. Canada and the British Army, 1846-1871. Revised. Toronto: University of Toronto Press for the Royal Commonwealth
Society, 1963.

Stacey, Charles Perry. The Canadian Army, 1939-1945. Ottawa: King's
Printer, 1948.

Stacey, Charles Perry. Quebec, 1759, the Siege and the Battle. Toronto:
Macmillan, 1959.

Stanley, George Francis Gilman. Canada's Soldiers: The Military History
of an Un-Military People. Toronto: Macmillan, 1960.

Tucker, Gilbert Norman. The Naval Service of Canada. Ottawa: King's
Printer, 1952.

Utter, William Thomas, et al. After Tippecanoe: Some Aspects of the
War of 1812. Toronto: Ryerson Press, 1963.

Wood, Herbert Fairlie. Strange Battleground: The Operations in Korea
and Their Effects on the Defence Policy of Canada. Ottawa: Queen's
Printer, 1966.

BIOGRAPHY

Bishop, Morris. Champlain, The Life of Fortitude. Toronto: McClelland
& Stewart, 1963.

Borden, Sir Robert Laird. Robert Laird Borden: His Memoirs. Toronto:
Macmillan, 1938.

Brady, Alexander. Thomas D'Arcy McGee. Toronto: Macmillan, 1925.

Campbell, Marjorie Wilkins. McGillivray, Lord of the Northwest. Toronto: Clarke, Irwin, 1962.

Careless, James Maurice Stockford. Brown of the Globe. Toronto:
Macmillan, 1960. 2 vols.

Cook, George Ramsay. The Politics of John W. Dafoe and the Free Press.
Toronto: University of Toronto Press, 1963.

Cooper, Leonard. Radical Jack: The Life of John George Lambton, Lord
Durham. London: Cresse, 1959.

Cox, Isaac Joselin. The Journeys of Réné Robert Cavalier, Sieur de la
Salle. New York: Allerton, 1922.

Creighton, Donald Grant. John A. Macdonald: The Young Politician.
Toronto: Macmillan, 1952.

Creighton, Donald Grant. John A. Macdonald: The Old Chieftain. Toronto:
Macmillan, 1955.

Dafoe, John Wesley. Sir Clifford Sifton in Relation to His Times. Toronto: Macmillan, 1931.

Davidson, William McCartney. Louis Riel, 1844-1885: A Biography.
Calgary: Albertan, 1955.

Dawson, Robert MacGregor. William Lyon Mackenzie King. Toronto:
University of Toronto Press, 1958.

Dictionary of Canadian Biography. Vol. 1-, 1000-1700-. Toronto: University of Toronto Press, 1966-. In progress.

Eccles, William John. Frontenac: The Courtier Governor. Toronto:
McClelland & Stewart, 1959.

Ferns, H. S., and B. Ostry. The Age of Mackenzie King & the Rise of the
Leader. London: Heinemann, 1955.

Flenley, Ralph. Samuel de Champlain. Toronto: Macmillan, 1924.

Glazebrook, George Parkin. Sir Charles Bagot in Canada: A Study in
British Colonial Government. Oxford: Clarendon Press, 1929.

Graham, Percy Wentworth. Sir Adam Beck. London, Ont.: Smith, 1925.

Graham, Roger. Arthur Meighen: A Biography. 3 vols. Toronto: Clarke,
Irwin, 1960-63.

Gray, John Morgan. Lord Selkirk of Red River. Toronto: Macmillan,
1963.

Harkness, Ross. J. E. Atkinson of the Star. Toronto: University of
Toronto Press, 1963.

Howe, Joseph. Joseph Howe: Voice of Nova Scotia: A Selection. Ed. J. Murray Beck. Toronto: McClelland & Stewart, 1964.

Hutchison, Bruce. The Incredible Canadian: A Candid Portrait of Mackenzie King. Toronto: Longmans, 1952.

Kilbourn, William. The Firebrand: William Lyon Mackenzie and the Rebellion in Upper Canada. Toronto: Clarke, Irwin, 1956.

Fraser, Simon. Letters and Journals. Ed. W. K. Lamb. Toronto: Macmillan, 1960.

Lichtenberger, André. Montcalm et la Tragedie Canadienne. Paris: Plon, 1934.

Longley, Ronald Stewart. Sir Francis Hincks: A Study of Canadian Politics, Railways and Finances in the Nineteenth Century. Toronto: University of Toronto Press, 1943.

McArthur, Peter. Sir Wilfrid Laurier. London: Dent, 1919.

MacGregor, Fred Alexander. The Fall and Rise of Mackenzie King, 1911-1919. Toronto: Macmillan, 1962.

McInnes, Grace. J. S. Woodsworth: A Man to Remember. Toronto: Macmillan, 1953.

McNaught, Kenneth William Kirkpatrick. A Prophet in Politics: A Biography of J. S. Woodsworth. Toronto: University of Toronto Press, 1959.

Marsh, D'Arcy Gilbert. The Tragedy of Henry Thornton. Toronto: Macmillan, 1935.

Massey, Vincent. What's Past is Prologue: The Memoirs of the Rt. Hon. Vincent Massey, C. H. London: Macmillan, 1963.

Montgomery, Richard Gill. The White Headed Eagle: John McLoughlin: Builder of an Empire. New York: Macmillan, 1935.

Morison, John Lyle. The Eighth Earl of Elgin: A Chapter in Nineteenth Century Imperial History. London: Hodder & Stoughton, 1928.

Morton, Arthur Silver. Sir George Simpson: Overseas Governor of the Hudson's Bay Company. Toronto: Dent, 1944.

Neatby, H. Blair. William Lyon Mackenzie King II: The Lonely Heights, 1924-1932. Toronto: University of Toronto Press, 1963.

New, Chester William. Lord Durham. Oxford: Clarendon Press, 1929.

Newman, Peter Charles. Renegade in Power: The Diefenbaker Years.
Toronto: McClelland & Stewart, 1963.

Osler, Edmund Boyd. The Man Who had to Hang: Louis Riel. Toronto:
Longmans, 1961.

Phelan, Josephine. The Ardent Exile: The Life and Times of Thomas
D'Arcy McGee. Toronto: Macmillan, 1951.

Pope, Joseph. Memoirs of the Right Hon. Sir John Alexander Macdonald.
Toronto: Macmillan, 1930.

Power, Charles Gavan. A Party Politician: The Memoirs of Chubby
Power. Ed. Norman Ward. Toronto: Macmillan, 1966.

Riddell, William Renwick. Life of John Graves Simcoe. Toronto: Mc-
Clelland & Stewart, 1926.

Roberts, Leslie. The Chief: A Political Biography of Maurice Duplessis.
Toronto: Clarke, Irwin, 1963.

Rolph, William Kirby. Henry Wise Wood of Alberta. Toronto: University
of Toronto Press, 1950.

Rumilly, Robert. Henri Bourassa. Montreal: Editions Chantecler, 1953.

Ryerson, Adolphus Egerton. The Story of My Life. Toronto: Briggs, 1883.

Sage, Walter Noble. Sir James Douglas and British Columbia. Toronto:
University of Toronto Press, 1930.

Saunders, Edward Manning. The Life and Letters of the Rt. Hon. Sir
Charles Tupper. New York: F. A. Stokes, 1916.

Schull, J. Laurier. Toronto: Macmillan, 1965.

Sissions, Charles Bruce. Egerton Ryerson: His Life and Letters.
Toronto: Clarke, Irwin, 1937-1947.

Skelton, Isabel. The Life of Thomas D'Arcy McGee. Gardenvale: Gardenvale City Press, 1925.

Skelton, Oscar Douglas. The Life and Letters of Sir Wilfrid Laurier.
Toronto: S. S. Grundy, 1921.

Skelton, Oscar Douglas. The Life and Times of Sir Alexander Tilloch Galt.
Toronto: Oxford University Press, 1920.

Stanley, George Francis Gillman. Louis Riel. Toronto: Ryerson Press,
1963.

Thompson, Edward John. The Life of Charles, Lord Metcalfe. London: Faber & Faber, 1937.

Thompson, Dale C. Alexander Mackenzie: Clear Grit. Toronto: Macmillan, 1960.

Tupper, Charles. Recollections of Sixty Years in Canada. London: Cassell, 1914.

Wallace, Elizabeth. Goldwin Smith: Victorian Liberal. Toronto: University of Toronto Press, 1957.

Watkins, Ernest. R. B. Bennett: A Biography. Toronto: British Book Service, 1963.

Wilson, George Earl. The Life of Robert Baldwin: A Study in the Struggle for Responsible Government. Toronto: Ryerson Press, 1933.

Wrong, Edward Murray. Charles Buller and Responsible Government. Oxford: Clarendon Press, 1926.

NAME INDEX

73954